NISSEN OF THE HUTS

A BIOGRAPHY OF LT COL PETER NISSEN DSO

Fred McCosh

1997

A B.D. PUBLISHING PUBLICATION

First published in 1997 by
B D Publishing
6 Wendover Road
BOURNE END, Bucks. SL8 5NT

British Library Cataloguing in Publication Data. A catalogue record for this book is available from the British Library.

McCosh F.W.J.
NISSEN OF THE HUTS:
A biography of Lt Col P N Nissen RE DSO
Inventor of the Nissen Hut.

ISBN 0 9525799 1 X

Cover artist - Mario
Typeset by B D Publishing, Bourne End, Bucks
Monochromes and Printing by Arrowhead Books Ltd, Reading, Berks.

To the memory of Olga Mary

1901 - 1991

By the same author

Boussingault:

Chemist and Agriculturist

(1984. Reidel, Dordrecht)

Fred W.J. McCosh was born in Woolwich in 1907. He studied chemistry and physics at Imperial College followed by a year at the London Day Training College. Most of his working career was spent in European and African schools in Rhodesia/Zimbabwe after which he obtained a PhD (London) in the History and Philosophy of Science. He has published articles on African traditional science whilst a research fellow at the University of Rhodesia/Zimbabwe.

CONTENTS

Peter Nissen is modelling the figure of a Royal Engineers Tunneller as part of the 1914-1918 war memorial to fallen members of the Institution of Mining and Metallurgy. Many of them were Tunnellers whose work was to lay and explode mines and to defuse those of the enemy. An electrical exploder is supported by a pile of sandbags.

(From the collection of P.C.M. Nissen)

LIST OF PLATES

LIST OF FIGURES

THE CHARACTERS

Georg Herman Nissen (1832-1913) father of Peter Norman Nissen

Annie Lavinia Nissen (née Fitch, 1842-c1930) Wife of Georg

Gurina Maria Nissen (Ena) (1869-1953) sister of

Reid Jones, neighbour of the Nissens at Thomasville, North Carolina

PETER NORMAN NISSEN (1871-1930)

Louisa Mair Nissen (née Richmond, 1873-1923) first wife of P N Nissen

Robert Richard Donger (1892-1952) Mechanical Draughtsman

Walter John Chamberlain (1869-1930) P N Nissen's Solicitor

Lauretta Nissen (née Maitland, 1882-1954) second wife of P N Nissen

William H Foulkes (? - 1944) Managing Director of Nissen Buildings Ltd

Chaim Schreiber (1918-1984) Furniture Manufacturer

PARTIAL GENEALOGICAL TABLE

THE NISSEN FAMILY

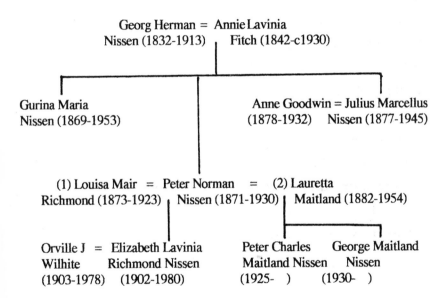

Georg Herman = Annie Lavinia
Nissen (1832-1913)   Fitch (1842-c1930)

Gurina Maria
Nissen (1869-1953)

Anne Goodwin = Julius Marcellus
(1878-1932)   Nissen (1877-1945)

(1) Louisa Mair = Peter Norman = (2) Lauretta
Richmond (1873-1923)   Nissen (1871-1930)   Maitland (1882-1954)

Orville J = Elizabeth Lavinia
Wilhite   Richmond Nissen
(1903-1978)   (1902-1980)

Peter Charles   George Maitland
Maitland Nissen   Nissen
(1925-)   (1930-)

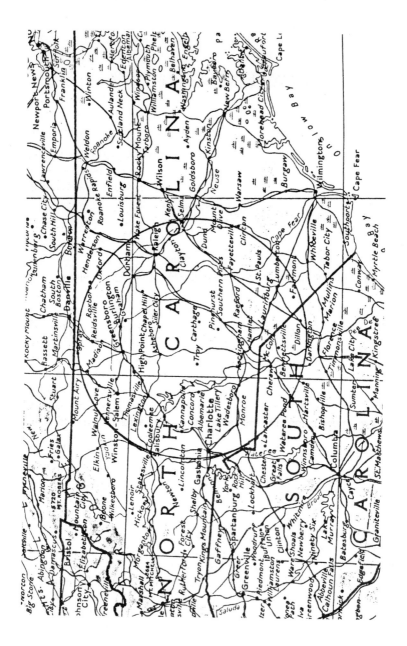

MAP OF NORTH CAROLINA. Towns mentioned in the text are within the circle e.g. Greensboro, High Point, Thomasville, Durham and Albemarle. Trinity College was sited 6 miles East of Thomasville. The diameter of the circle represents a distance of about 150 miles. (Adapted from The Oxford Atlas (OUP 1951, page 91. Courtesy of Oxford University Press.)

HOW IT BEGAN

'To be is to be perceived'
George Berkeley, 1713, *Three
Dialogues between Hylas and Philonous*

"Success is not just about talent:
It's about image and coverage.'
Sub-headline in *The Independent*

Is it true that the Nissen Hut was invented by a Japanese car manufacturer? This is the received view of many, which may explain why Lt. Col. Peter Norman Nissen has become one of this century's talented unknowns. Large families in African society may guarantee a supply of manual labour but they also ensure that the ancestor is not forgotten. Perhaps the greatest fear of an African is the possibility that at some time his name and reputation will be remembered by nobody and so his spirit falls into the limbo of the forgotten, a fate without parallel. In the more impersonal society of the West an audience is needed, rather than a family, to maintain a knowledgeable appreciation of the artist and the achievement. Bishop Berkeley could hardly have imagined today's extension of his 'perceived' to the global television broadcasts of today where 'image' and 'coverage' appear to be the necessary catalysts for the recognition of talent. If only 'NISSEN' had been moulded on steel for the huts just as 'NISSAN' appears on the tailboards of vans and trucks !

It was known that Nissen once lived on Westerham Hill. The *Westerham and Crockham Hill Guide* devotes two and a half lines to him in a chapter on 'Westerham and its People', whereas General James Wolfe receives fifteen and Sir Winston Churchill eleven lines. How difficult to achieve fame in the presence of such giants ! My curiosity was further aroused by Beryl Kallend who lives at 'Deepdale', the house on Westerham Hill where Nissen lived for the last eight years of his life. Mrs Kallend mentioned to my wife at a Women's Institute meeting that there was still some ironwork on her property which belonged to Nissen. And so it started from there.

Whilst assembling a biography of one who died in 1930 I am reminded of the varying quantity of documentary and oral information available at different periods of time. The Victorians and those long before them kept diaries, wrote letters and hoarded those received, leaving a miscellany of archival material awaiting the attention of the biographer. Yet oral evidence after such a lapse of time may be minimal or even lacking. As a contrast, those recently dead have left a verbal library of thoughts, sayings and ideas readily expressed by their family, friends and colleagues. Between these two groups are those who have died within memory of the very old, and such is the case with my subject. One had been an errand boy for the local butcher, but had contact only with Nissen's servants. Another vaguely recollects playing with a Nissen son when both were about five years, and whose aunt Jay was a 'nanny' to the Nissen children. And that was all !

Were there not two Nissen sons as mentioned in *Who was Who* ? No progress had been made in locating them until I met Elizabeth Hoath in the churchyard of St Mary the Virgin, Westerham. Staring despondently at the Nissen grave and bemoaning my lack of success, I was soon to discover that she is a mine of local history. A member of the Family Name Society, she enquired from Sheila Humphreys of Keston who in turn contacted Jill Valentine of Hayes who replied that her husband worked for the same finance house in the City of London as George Nissen, the younger son. This was a tremendous break-through and I am most grateful to these three ladies. Soon I was writing to Peter Charles Nissen, the elder son and a meeting was arranged in London. A file of manuscripts by Nissen's widow Lauretta was entrusted to me and soon there arose the concept of a book rather than the article which was originally envisaged.

"My dear children" (wrote Lauretta), "sometimes when your father and I were sitting talking at 'Deepdale' I used to say to him, 'If anything were to happen to you, I should hardly know anything about you to tell Peter, you must write down the chief events of your life.' Well, he didn't do it and as you know he left us so suddenly it seemed impossible to believe he wasn't there to answer any more questions. So I am now trying to put

14

down all the little things he did tell me so that you may have a faint conception of what life meant for him."

Lauretta Nissen was not the only member of that family with an archival instinct. Another, yet larger harvest of papers, photographs, letters and files awaited me at our next meeting which not only extended the range of this biography but corrected various errors arising from the reading of faulty obituary notices - such as whether Nissen was born in Canada, New York, North Carolina or California ? I am most grateful to Peter Charles Nissen and George Maitland Nissen for their interest and encouragement in the project.

This book would never have appeared but for the information volunteered by a host of institutions and people from whom I made enquiries. They include the Institution of Mining and Metallurgy, (Michael Carr), the Ministry of Defence (Judith Blacklaw), Queen's University, Kingston, Ontario (Anne MacDermaid and especially Paul Banfield), Dalane Folkemuseum Egersund, Anne Ulset and Kari Hoseth Peters for Norwegian translation, Hull Central Library, Imperial War Museum, The District Councils of South Somerset, Orkney and Broxbourne, Barlow Rand Ltd. (Diana Arnott), Strange Library Johannesburg (Carol Leigh), Kamftuppenschule I Hammelburg, Theresa and Thomas Rouvrey for German translation, Karim Arafat for Greek and Arabic translation, Peter Donger and Ken Willetts whose fathers were pioneer employees of Nissen Buildings Ltd., and especially Maurice Fox a former employee who sent me detailed notes, the Australian High Commission London (Athalie Colquhoun), Tony Kallend of 'Deepdale', Royal Engineers Library Chatham (especially Margaret Magnuson), Church of the Holy Angels, Hounslow (Eric Beales), Companies House at Cardiff, the Patents Offices of Canada, South Africa, United States and United Kingdom; Croydon Local Studies Library (Steve Round), Lincoln's Inn Library (Guy Holborn), Mineral Industries Educational Trust (Glynne Lloyd-Davis), MFI (Hamish Thomson), Chamber of Mines of South Africa (P. Bunell), Anglo-American Corporation of South Africa, English Heritage (Dr Martin Cherry), Roy Fido, British Library Newspaper Library, Mike Burrows, LUTCHI Research Centre University of Lougborough (especially Linda Candy), Graham Morris and Schreiber Industries Ltd., the Kent County Library at Westerham (Fiona Robbins) and many others who have kindly answered my enquiries, or have guided me by hint or word in the direction of new material for this book, my warm thanks to them all.

Except for those, now senior citizens, who found shelter and comfort in his huts during World War II, or more recently in the Falklands, 'Nissen' fails to recall the inventor, especially among the younger generation. It appears that a biography is more readable if the subject has been involved in some form of controversy the details of which were known at the time by the general public. Political, social, financial and artistic controversies have always existed but not to the extent that they do today, encouraged by press rewards and the services of 'moles' who reveal the secrets of those who employ them. Nor was there a newspaper editor who felt it was in the 'public interest' to reveal the differences between Nissen and the accepted authorities of his time. There was the Nissen mining stamp against which technical objections were raised by mine managers in South Africa; then the Nissen hut which had its critics among the professionals of the Royal Engineers, especially when the hut was given his name, followed by a peace-time wrangle with the United Kingdom Government, first as to a suitable reward for the invention, and then over the unpaid royalties on government hut sales. Such controversies occurred long before the media ever claimed that 'the public demands to know the facts !' which, I suggest. accounts partly for his present day anonymity.

Today's advanced means of communication allow the pursuit of a career in several dimensions and on several continents, yet Nissen accomplished this in the first three decades of the century when, as a mining engineer, inventor, soldier and industrialist, the world was truly his oyster !

The author must take full responsibility for any errors of fact or presentation.

Westerham, Kent.   F.W.J. McC.
August 1997

1. PIONEERS ! O PIONEERS !

'Much have I travelled in the realms of gold
And many goodly states and kingdoms seen
(Keats: "On first looking into Chapman's Homer")

Irrelevant lines you may think, on starting a biography of a practical man, living among practical people. But wait ! I am writing first about Georg Herman Nissen, father of *Nissen of the Huts*, and about the middle of a family of eleven children, who exchanged his native Norway for the better life which many desired, but few at first found, in the United States of the mid-nineteenth century. It was for many a cliff-hanging experience on a thin strip of arid country clinging to the Scandinavian massif. Families sending their sons to sea, to fish or to man boats that plied to a New World, bringing back tales of a new and better life overseas, free from the domination of Dane or Swede.

I find it extraordinary that Norway was prevented from becoming a sovereign state until 1905, recent history to me, born only two years later. Even a cursory reading of Scandinavian history forms the impression that Norway for centuries was a commercial and political shuttlecock in a game between Denmark and Sweden. Or perhaps a complicated saga in which each of the three countries yearns to dominate the other two, where Norway is the perpetual loser ? The seed of discontent was sown at the Union of Kalmar as far back as 1397 because of a false assumption that they were tied by a similar language and culture. To paraphrase an Oscar Wilde quip about the United States and the United Kingdom, 'Three great countries divided by a common language !" Norway's climb to sovereignty began with the Treaty of Kiel in 1814 when Denmark was forced to abandon Norway because of Danish support for Napoleon: and finished with the Treaty of Karlstad in 1905 when Sweden relinquished its political hold as a result of Norway's threatened resistance to a Swedish armed invasion. The Nissen's hatred of Denmark during the nineteenth century seems odd as they originated from that country. A Nissen family legend relates how an ancestor melted down his table silver to provide funds to equip a Norwegian army against a threatened Danish occupation, but dating the incident proves difficult. It is known that the original family home was a farm which they then owned at Bov Sogn on an island of South Jutland on which Copenhagen stands.

One of the family, Mado, having sailed as a mate for several years, was appointed in 1794 as Commissioner of Customs at Egersund, a small port south of Stavanger, and from that time the Nissen family regarded themselves as Norwegians. But Egersund reminds us of small Scottish coastal towns, which before the advent of the North Sea oil industry were beset by trade recessions followed by promises of new industries which did not always fulfil expectations. Shipping by sail collapsed when neighbouring ports took to steamers: then a herring oil factory which could only operate in Spring; but the Egersund pottery, until it closed in 1979, provided employment for over one hundred years. Perhaps not an attractive town to the tourist which probably explains why I failed to find a mention of it in the usual guides. But it was Georg Herman Nissen's town which he left to be apprenticed to a carpenter in Bergen, obtaining an 'advanced craft certificate' which suggests that he attended a technical school there. This is a history of Scandinavia, all too brief and simplistic, covering six centuries, but a necessary background to Georg's perambulations in North America.

The saga of Georg's emigration to the United States is more a part of family folk-lore that reality. His port of embarkation and arrival there are as little known as his reason for leaving Norway. The legend is that his father, Peder Nissen, knew a Scotsman, Donald Mackay, shipbuilder of Boston, Massachusetts, and it was to Mackay that the young Georg was to be sent to learn shipbuilding. We know nothing of the voyage except that the boat left Norway in 1857, the voyage took two weeks but a further two were to pass before passengers could land because of head winds which prevented the boat from berthing ! Another story maintains that he left Norway in 1850 and quickly followed in the tracks of the 'forty-niners' on their way to the Californian gold-field. A more likely report is that the boat sailed up the St Lawrence river and docked either at Quebec or Ottawa from whence he travelled to Chicago. Boston never saw him for another ten years. A possible proof of his arrival at Chicago is found in his United States Certificate of Citizenship, granted to him in 1889 in which is pencilled '1857 Chicago'. Perhaps Georg wrote this important date to remind him when he was applying for citizenship for although he had a memory for mining contracts completed he appeared weak on dates. Had the Californian gold-field account been correct we would have expected a report of the treacherous route over the Rockies, across the Utah desert and the climb over the Sierra Nevadas, a route signposted by skeletons of pack animals, and even humans, lured to their deaths by the prospect of gold. And all this on a pony which was to be bought in Boston ? Fortunately, in later years, his daughter, Gurina, urged him to write an account of his travels. The pencilled record was carefully preserved by Gurina and so here is the first part of Georg's journeyings, which never included the Boston shipyard. Was it the lure of gold or merely an objection to another apprenticeship ?

"I am a native of Norway. I came to the United States in 1857 and left Chicago in the Spring of 1858 for Fort Leavenworth, Kansas, in the fall of the same year I went to Missouri where I was engaged in contracting for and building houses."

"In the Spring of 1860 I left for Pike's Peak where I remained until 1867. During my period of residence in Colorado I was engaged in mining and erecting mining machinery. I did a great deal of mechanical work, viz. - I built two of the largest overshot wheels in Colorado. I built two blowing cylinders for smelters and a couple of furnaces, which was the first smelter put up in that State. I also built several stamp-mills...... I left Colorado in 1867 for Boston where I was engaged as a pattern-maker in the Boston Machine Works. In the Spring of 1868 I went to Nova Scotia. I was engaged by a party for one year to go there and open a mine and to build a ten-stamp-mill. This I did and afterwards took contracts for erecting stamp-mills. Three stamp-mills I built in Goldenville and following that I built a ten-stamp-mill in Louistown and one in Country Harbour. I left Nova Scotia in the Spring of 1870 for New York where I remained until 1878......."

This purely workaday report does not end there but is resumed when he sets up home in North Carolina. Astounding though is the magnitude of the tasks he completed - truly one of the early builders of the industrial United States ! Stamp-mills became his speciality, those automatic crushers of gold ore, like a row of pile drivers. Stamp-mills will henceforth appear in my story as characters in the mining activities of the Nissen family. With almost a one-track mind, the milestones of life were the stamp-mills which he built throughout the United States and Canada.

I believe I can make sense out of this jigsaw of fact and myth about Georg's wanderings. It is known that a small party en route for the Californian gold field had camped at Fort Leavenworth in 1849 where they had found gold in the local rock. Warned by an Indian chief that snow was falling on the Sierra Nevada where many, California bound, had frozen to death, the party delayed their departure until the following Spring leaving Georg at Fort Leavenworth. Perhaps disappointed with their Californian claims they returned to Fort Leavenworth in 1858 to further develop their claims of 1849. By that time Georg had some claims there which he refused to sell when offers were made during the American Civil War of 1861-65. Miners, the majority of them, believed that the Confederate forces of the southern states would triumph and that consequently northern money would be valueless. A great pity, because in 1863-64, when miners were willing to sell, there were no takers because the reef was now yielding pyritic ore, gold containing iron pyrites or 'fools gold' which demanded a costlier extraction process. How technology and politics can prove incompatible bedfellows ! At the same time he appears to have been in the 'cross-fire' between rival Indian tribes when he was taken hostage but rescued by the opposition, taken 'to the Nebeska' (Nebraska perhaps) and after several days without food he was sustained by a soup prepared from potato skins ! But this was not the end; he was photographed with a number of Indian chiefs. Disappointing that this example of early photography has disappeared, but his daughter Gurina, later confirmed that she had seen the print.

Perhaps disgusted with his Fort Leavenworth failure, he was off to St Joseph Missouri, driving a wagon of provisions including a load of potatoes and flour. From what Nissen told his wife Lauretta at 'Deepdale', Westerham, years after, 'the wagon separated in a river......and all these precious things were lost'. Did these setbacks determine the move northwards to Pike's peak, west of the present day tourist centre of Colorado Springs, or was he distancing himself from the Civil War ?

As much as a bachelor in the nineteenth century Colorado could call any place his home, Georg settled at Pike's Peak for about seven years, and this, I suggest was his 'technical college' when in a practical manner he consolidated his experience gained at Fort Leavenworth and completed his unofficial apprenticeship to become a mining engineer. Yet even Pike's Peak could not hold him forever and in the wake of a mini-gold rush at Goldenville in Nova Scotia he left, first for a short spell of pattern making in Boston, then on to Nova Scotia. Georg Nissen was now 35 years and still unmarried. The primitive conditions of mining camps may have deterred him from seeking a wife ? ; but the more civilised Nova Scotia was a turning point. 'In the Spring of 1868 I went to Nova Scotia' - runs the report. Not mentioned was that on April 9th, still 'the Spring of 1868' he married Annie Lavinia Fitch, but we hear nothing of this whirlwind romance the speed of which may have raised doubts for Annie's father, Elisha, who objected to his daughter marrying a 'foreigner'. The Marriage notice in *The Halifax Reporter* of April 14th gives rise to some interesting queries - ' ....At the residence of the bride's father.....' - what had happened to Annie's mother ? And the bridegroom was George Hamlin Nissen Esq. of Christiana, Norway' surely written by some cub reporter making up his column without checking the facts ? And 'Christiana' indeed ! Was this an intentional slip of the tongue ? Or, in a bemused moment, had he leaked that his boat of 1857 had embarked from Christiana, todays Oslo ? Just as interesting is the baptismal record of their first child, Gurina, in February 1869 where Georg's occupation is given as 'shoemaker'. Pattern-maker, house-builder and now shoemaker, a diversity of trades which guaranteed employment for Georg between stamp-mill commissions, employment which now helped to support the stable household which had replaced his former bachelor existence.

Annie Fitch came of pioneer stock, descended from James Fitch of Essex who with his wife Abigail sailed for the New World in 1635 in the ship *Defence* and settled in Connecticut. This was only fifteen years after the *Mayflower* set sail from Plymouth. Politically the Fitch family had long been Union-Loyalists or 'Uni-Loyalists' as they were called, for they were loyal to the British Government and had no desire to become Americans. This may appear a selfish and negative manifesto, especially as many immigrants were now enjoying a better life-style then their contemporaries in Britain. Yet the Uni-Loyalists had so far no legally constituted country to which they could demonstrate their allegiance; the term 'America' meant only a loose

21

combination of thirteen states each of which tended to become independent of the others. The loyalty of the Fitch family was shared by about one third of the population of these states who either fought alongside the British armies in the American War of Independence of 1774-76, or were neutral, or just 'Loyalists'. In all three groups there were those, the victims of draconian punishments, who lost their jobs, their houses and businesses; banned from claiming damages due to mob violence; double and treble taxes levied, and in some states there was no legal redress against such acts. To those who wished to leave America the British Government offered farms in various parts of the world including Nova Scotia where the Fitch family finally settled. In later years, in choosing England for his home, Peter Nissen paid tribute to his mother Annie who created in him a love and respect for England, its countryside and its customs.

A wanderer ever, Georg Nissen left Nova Scotia in 1870 for New York where the family stayed for about eight years whilst Georg was employed as a pattern-maker once again, with family responsibilities demanding a steady income. And so we complete the 'irrelevant' lines at the beginning of the chapter:

'Or like stout Cortez when with eagle eyes
He star'd at the Pacific......
Silent upon a peak in Darien'

or was it Balboa who first saw the Pacific ? -
which brings us back to Georg likewise observing the Chicago end of a mighty country from the deck of a Norwegian clipper fourteen years ago, but not as a Walt Whitman stereotype:

'Follow well in order, get your weapons ready,
Have you your pistols ? Have you sharp-edged axes ?
Pioneers ! O Pioneers !

but like others from Europe he came to carve out a career in a continent where standards of democracy were superior to the class-conscious attitudes of their mother countries. Without this preliminary chapter on Georg Herman Nissen it might be difficult to appreciate why Peter Nissen followed in his father's pioneer footsteps in an America which had developed to some degree of

22

industrial sophistication with a wider variety of occupations open to him, but with hindsight we recognise that it was the obvious path in a family moving from mine to mine.

Sources agree that Peter Norman Nissen was born on August 6th 1871, but where ? Of the various suggestions made in the obituaries the two which can claim veracity are New York and North Carolina, either of which confirms citizenship of the USA. Perhaps we can dismiss as trivial the remark of a reporter from a Pittsburgh newspaper who met him in France in 1916, 'I knew he was an American by the way he said, 'Hello'.' *The family Nissen of Bov Sogn in South Sjaelland* (Trondheim 1978), a translation of the Norwegian title, claims New York as his birthplace, whereas the gravestone in Westerham churchyard is engraved 'North Carolina' without stating the actual place. Perhaps the only reliable source would have been Elizabeth Lavinia Nissen (1902-1982), daughter of the first marriage. However, the third and last child, Julius, was born in Philadelphia in 1877 after which Georg had a contract in Georgia, and then in North Carolina. In spite of much verbal agreement that Peter Nissen was born in North Carolina there is evidence that he was born in New York. Neither claim, North Carolina or New York, can be sustained by registries of births and deaths as those at New York and in North Carolina did not exist in 1871 nor were they generally established in the United Kingdom until 1837.

My birthplace vote goes to New York as it fits in well with subsequent moves.

The Hornblende Mill at Wawa, Ontario, built by Nissen in 1899. It was a 2-stamp mill and the first Nissen Stamp Mill to be installed. (from the collection of P.C.M. Nissen.)

24

2. CAROLINA DAYS

'I am the people, humble, hungry, mean -
Hungry yet today despite the dream
Beaten yet today - O Pioneers !
I am the man who never got ahead'
(Langston Hughes - 'Let America be America Again')

Georg Nissen never fitted this description but the son of such a pioneer became President of the United States - Abraham Lincoln ! Georg had saved sufficiently to leave New York and return to Norway with wife Annie and two children, Gurina and young Peter in 1873 to find that his mother had died but his father at 75 was still living. Georg returned to New York in advance of the family, filling his free time with toy-making for the returning children who themselves brought back a dolls' house made by their Norwegian grandfather. Gurina reports, 'When we returned from Europe we brought with us a tremendous packing case holding a dolls' house my grandfather, Peder, had made for me, an exact replica of a coffee house that was in my great-grandfather's grounds - the one that had the glass bells in the trees. It had six dolls and the roof of the ceiling where the cupola came on was of tin so a small chandelier hanging could have the candles burning. The big box was iron bound, with handles and for many years was used as a packing case for linen and blankets in our travels - of course the house was there too.' I have doubts whether Peter, at 1½ years, really appreciated a dolls' house ? He was learning to speak and of course, prattled in Norwegian which baffled his small friends in New York, calling him 'little Dutchman' which he angrily denied with 'I ikke Dutch' (I not Dutch). The family, once more united, contemplated another series of inexplicable moves, first to Philadelphia, where Julius, their third child was born, thence to Georgia, finally settling at High Point in North Carolina. Regrettably, Georg was born far too late to take advantage of North Carolina's 'golden age' when, before 1829, all gold mined in the United States came from this State.

Now for a little history. After Spain had unsuccessfully attempted to establish a colony there in the early 16th century it was Raleigh in 1587 who settled English emigrants in what was then Virginia which included the present day North Carolina. A Roger Green was granted a vast area of land which became North Carolina by legislation in 1653. Thereafter, French Huguenots, who had been living in Virginia, crossed the border to settle in North Carolina in 1700, soon followed by waves of immigrants from Ireland, Scotland, Wales, Germany and England, a suitable mixture to give an 'Englishness' to the State. But in spite of the establishment of a university or perhaps because of it, North Carolina developed a state of political and economic torpor lasting the first third of the 19th century, and indeed, it was known as the 'Rip Van Winkle' state after Washington Irving's character who slept for twenty years. The lack of constructive policy, both public and private, compared sadly with States such as New York, Pennsylvania, Virginia and even South Carolina !

I find it remarkable, in an historical sense, that Nissen, who died about sixty years ago and was therefore possibly known to several old people today, should have lived his boyhood in the strained and unhappy aftermath of the American Civil War of 1861-65. Tenuous connections perhaps by small boys and youths now in their seventies and eighties but expressive of the continuity of time. The Northern and Southern States had been on a collision course for many years whilst two vastly different industrial revolutions had been developing and diverging. In the North an increasing tendency towards mass production resulted from the inventiveness of Eli Whitney and others by which the unskilled could be taught to assemble complicated machinery due to the standardisation of machine parts.

It began the era of assembly line production and the division of labour at a time of skilled labour shortage and thus industry took over from handicrafts in an urban industrial revolution. In the Southern States Whitney had also made his mark. His cotton gin replaced hand-picking of seeds from the lint. Instead of employing twenty slaves to pick and clean twenty pounds of cotton each day the gin enabled the farmer to plant more and more cotton provided he could recruit more slaves. Not only cotton but sugar and tobacco farmers demanded an increased labour force for the enormous estates of the South, forming a rural industrial revolution unrelated to that of the North except through expanding transport systems which brought the two cultures face to face with slavery, the dominant divider. America progressively became an area of conflict in which the President, Abraham Lincoln, during four bloody years of war, stood solidly for the supremacy of the American State which could only be obtained by the abolition of slavery, effected by an Act of Congress in January 1865.

Although an official peace prevailed, there were regions where opinion about slavery was deeply divided. There were those who wished to remain neutral like the Cornish miners who were employed at the newly found gold strikes in Rowan County North Carolina, from 1858; their neutrality was not appreciated and they were greeted with cries of 'You damned Britishers !' as a result of which they joined the Confederate Army of the Southern States but resigned when wounded and dead were returned from the battlefront. It was to this devastated State of North Carolina, its young men decimated by war, that Georg and Annie Nissen brought their family. North Carolina had been reluctant to enter the war, its Governor had resisted the order of the Southern States president to apply conscription and to suspend *habeas corpus* and resisted also the demand for military supplies. In the end, the 'burnt-earth' strategy of General Sherman, 'from Atlanta to the sea', decided the end of the war, but not before Sherman had captured Georgia and South Carolina and was about to enter North Carolina. Lauretta Nissen, quoting her husband's recollections of his early days, wrote:

"Peter Nissen was born seven years after the end of the great Civil War between the North and South of America so although all the negroes he knew were free men, many of them must originally have been slaves. Even by the time Peter was old enough to talk and listen intelligently the war was still recent enough to leave a deep shadow, and the the part of the country where he lived had not recovered from the ruin and disorganisation which followed the war. Not only were the negroes very poor, but the 'Poor Whites' lived a very miserable existence and many families which had once been rich and important must have been living in a very small way."

Apart from Nissen's recollections of life in North Carolina, much interesting information came from a near neighbour, Reid Jones who was two years Nissen's junior, and met him in 1883 when the family moved from High Point to Thomasville where the Nissens and the Jones lived on adjacent plots. Reid Jones writes:

"In the South following the Civil War the construction years business had been all but destroyed and the flower of young manhood had been pretty well wiped out during the year so that the country even in the 80's had made little progress towards recovery and money was still pretty scarce, for this reason the schools were few and far between and it was only the favoured few that got a chance to get more than a common school education. I, unfortunately, was not among those favoured few and for this reason I have little I can say about our school days. My brother and sister who were older than I were more fortunate. There was a girls' College in the village but none for young men...."

His letter confirms the general opinion that the Civil war transformed a progressive and prosperous North Carolina in 1860 into the divided, defeated and exhausted State of 1865, most of the young men killed, as many of the young soldiers were only sixteen years of age, and thousands returned disabled. His reference to a girls College concerns the Greensboro Female College, the result of an unusual but distinct movement in the Southern States to establish Colleges for girls, each of which maintained a preparatory department corresponding to a secondary school. In North Carolina many of these Colleges were financed by the Methodist Church, similar to the establishment of schools by missions in former British colonial territories before government subsidised them out of general taxation.

Enough of history for the moment and back to the family, Georg and his wife Annie, daughter Gurina and sons Peter and Julius. Because he was in charge of gold mines in North Carolina Georg preferred a residence near his work which meant an occasional change of address, first High Point, then Thomasville followed by Albemarle, small towns or villages in those days but now large enough to be identified in a general atlas. To be near your current goldmine did necessitate a move of residence, as Nissen later explained to his wife Lauretta, because Georg rode to work or went in a wagon with his own horses along poor roads when sometimes the wagon would have to be prized out of the mud. Such moves may have accounted for the long absences from school during which young Nissen accompanied his father to the mines.

My intended chapter heading was to have been 'Carolina Paradise', for that was my reaction to Lauretta NIssen's account of life in North Carolina as told by her husband Peter. Nostalgic recollections may flatteringly embroider

28

the truth but even so, there is here a tale of almost bucolic living, at least for the younger generation, of an era devoid of automobiles and television. Lauretta continues:

"The Nissens had evidently a fair sized piece of ground and kept cows, horses, pigs, chickens and I know that they had a goat at one time.... The children had a goat carriage, Gurina says, 'Out turn-out was most elaborate, such a lovely wagon and the harness was so grand, father had it all made for us....I know that I learned to ride horseback down in a meadow and of course almost all we ate was grown'. Peter used to tell me he could take the cows to pasture when he was five and milk them when he was eight.... One little incident had a profound effect on Peter. He had borrowed an old gun from a boy friend and to his dismay it broke. In great distress he went to his father who only said, 'Oh broken is it, well then why don't you mend it ?' Peter carried off the gun and proceeded to take it to pieces. He found a small part broken in two. He got a piece of metal and a file and worked away until he had made a piece exactly like the broken part. Then he put the gun together again and to his great delight it worked as well as ever". Games and activities form an interesting list, played by the three of them, Peter, Julius and Reid. What were the rules, I wonder, of Town-ball. One old cat, Two old cat ? But I recognise baseball, marbles, fishing and flying kites. Living off the land meant the gathering of wild grapes, blackberries, sundew berries and without detailed explanation there was 'frog-hunting', and in the fall they gathered hickory nuts, walnuts and locust fruits - the beans from the Corob or Locust tree of the Mediterranean which I recollect in my childhood in London. Reid Jones continues his long letter to Lauretta Nissen:-

"Also in the early Winter we would make our rabbit traps or rabbit gums as they were called in those days in that particular part of the country due to the fact that sometimes they were made out of hollow gum trees...... In those days there was very little, if any, coal burned as we were so far from the coal fields. Besides, wood was plentiful and it was universally used for heating purposes, this wood would be cut in eight feet lengths in the forests and brought that way to the homes. So it was up to the men-folk or boys of every household to cut wood to the proper length for the fireplace or store as the case may be. The furnaces or steam houses were practically unknown (I think he means hot waters systems.) So Peter, Julius and I would help each other cut up his wood. I would help them and they in turn would help me, this made it seem more like play than work......Peter used to make napkin rings out of gum wood, the bark being rough and the wood white, he would hollow these out and polish them, and varnish the outside and then send them north and sell them. They were very artistic looking...."

'Now as to things we ate in those days. I imagine about the same as you have in your country, beef, mutton, pork, bacon, sausages, turkeys (domestic and wild) rabbits, quail and all kinds of fish, frog-legs, ducks, and some did, and do yet, eat opossum, mostly blacks. Perhaps you don't have sweet potatoes, sometimes called 'yams'. All kinds of fruits, water-melons, mush-melons, (a soft melon ?) cantaloupes, honey-dew melons, plums, cherries, apricots, apples, peaches, strawberries. raspberries and various kinds of grapes one of which is known as the Scuppernong (after the river of that name in North Carolina), it is a very large grape which is almost a tan colour when quite ripe and very delicious, and the wine from this grape, when properly made, has almost a champagne taste as the grape is peculiar to the Southern States....We also have muscadines (a large black grape) and several kinds of wild grapes. Our oranges, grapefruit, tangerines, etc., we have to get from Florida, Texas or California.' Matching this Carolinean cornucopia of natural foods with the excellent health of the Nissen family reminds me of a remark due to Anthelme Brillat-Severin, a French gastronome who, in his 1826 volume on the physiology of taste stated, 'Man is what he eats !', surely a fundamental tenet of healthy and civilised eating ?

So Reid Jones sent a long, rambling list of activities, games and eatables known to the North Carolinians in the latter half of the 19th century. Some of the children's games, Town ball, One old cat, Two old cats, are unknown to me, and I am surprised that there is no mention of 'jacks' or 'jacky fivestones' which has a long history, played as it was originally with small rounded pebbles or 'jackstones'. As for the catalogue of meats and fruits I can only conclude that immigration and air-cargoes have enabled the otherwise conservative British to sample exotic foods, little known to them in such vast quantities that young Nissen and his friends enjoyed. Altogether a happy and most satisfactory pastoral scene of a closely-knit family life, each one of whom knew their place and function in the domestic organisation.

Whether they were living at High Point, Thomasville or Albemarle, we hear nothing of poor health or disease but the record was seriously marred on one occasion when Georg suffered as a result of a mine accident, as told by Lauretta:

'He was just leaving the mine to go home when his attention was drawn to something that was not running right and, in stooping over, his coat was caught and he was revolved round the shaft a great many times before the machinery could be stopped. With great presence of mind he kept his head in such a position that he was uninjured, but his arm was badly shattered. To find the doctor he then walked over a mile and got over a rail fence holding his broken arm close to his side with his good arm. Gurina says, 'I do remember so clearly seeing him in bed in a hotel and his poor arm was so yellow and swollen I cried and cried. I was so shocked. It was a perfectly good arm afterwards and he had no ill effects from it.'

Georg was obviously a tough character to withstand such a horrific experience, but there is evidence that his bones were brittle for this was his third arm fracture. As a baby he fell from a couch to the floor breaking his arm. Then as a boy he lost his grip on the well handle at Egersund, the filled bucket fell rapidly whilst the rotating handle, out of control, repeatedly struck his arm breaking it, so it is said, in eleven places ! Luaretta continues the list of fractures:

"The children realised that their father was an utterly fearless man. He had lost the third finger and part of the little finger on his left hand and I am sure I remember Peter telling me that his father had to chop off his own finger with a hatchet to free it !" presumably when trapped in machinery.

Their mother, Annie, took advantage of the plethora of food and was rated an excellent cook by the family and neighbours, although expressing a dislike of cooking. Nissen in after years recollected his mother's lamb stew with 'crackers' soaked in gravy. Neighbour Reid Jones too thought her doughnuts and cinnamon buns 'were a joy to a kid's taste..... and the aroma from her kitchen would make you hungry though you had just eaten.' Yet Annie knew almost nothing about cooking until she was married - was this perhaps the result of employing a negro cook in her father's home in Nova Scotia ? But she also learned to cure meat and smoke hams in barrels with hickory chips.

One might naturally ponder how such children as the Nissens, living in a New World 'Eden', would react to present day circumstances to, among others, such features as the pressure of road traffic, the media, and, in many cases, to the lack of parental guidance in discriminating between right and wrong ? A too complicated question which I shall dodge and plead that time spent on surmising the responses of children just over a hundred years ago to the restraints of present day life would be non-productive. Instead, I shall reproduce an incident which was relevant in those days, if not ours, and leave the story without unnecessary comment before closing the chapter and embarking on Peter Nissen's 'education', a subject more exciting than the term connotes. The speaker, again, Reid Jones:

'....., one morning, Peter, Julius and several other children had a calf in a push cart taking it out to pasture about two miles away and after they got there they were going to release the calf and spend the remainder of the day picking berries and having a generally good time. They stopped in front of our house and asked me to join them and you can imagine how crazy I was to go but my mother said 'No !' that I had to churn so I sorrowfully broke the news to them and they went on, and about that time my mother put the milk in the churn and then a bright idea struck me. So I started churning and churned as no boy before or since has churned. I know I broke the world's record and my mother said I could go. So I ran as hard as my feet would let me and caught them up before they got to the pasture. So we had a grand reunion and I was one happy lad and we had one happy day, and one that all concerned didn't think possible when my mother said I had to churn first.'

3. A SINGULAR ENGINEER

No account of Peter Nissen's education would be complete without noting the rise of Trinity College, North Carolina, to university status, because he was part of it, if only for several years. Few people nowadays appear to have heard of a 1920 biography of James Abram Garfield, twentieth President of the United States entitled *From Log Cabin to White House*, yet the rise of Trinity College could be described as 'From Leaky Log Cabin to World Acclaimed University', this last being Duke University in Durham, North Carolina.

Needless to say, there were no Parent-Teacher Associations in the rural areas of North Carolina - the parents were the teachers ! The children, when not employed on the farm, were taught the three Rs by their parents, probably the mothers, until parents made use of 'wandering schoolmasters' for whom they later built 'schoolhouses' in which their children could be taught. In about 1830 one such schoolhouse was built by John Brown on his plantation. 'Browns Schoolhouse', as it became known, made of round logs and only 16 feet by 20 feet in size, was taken over by the Rev. Brantly York, a Minister of the Methodist Episcopal Church who vividly described the school as it was in 1837:

'..... a schoolhouse built of round logs, and covered with common boards. The floor was laid with puncheons (short wood posts ?) and slabs. The chimney was made of wood with little or no clay in it....The hearth was dirt, and the whole in bad repair; for when it rained, it was with difficulty that the books and paper could be kept dry. The house was entirely too small to accommodate the students, consequently we were necessitated to erect a brush arbor in front of the south door, and part of the students were under the arbor and part in the house.' The 'brush arbor' seems likely to have been a lean-to greenhouse formed from young trees trained over a trellis.

A new schoolhouse was built, 20 feet by 30 feet, but this was soon too small for the fast increasing number of children in the district as the understatement of the year suggests - '......York experienced considerable difficulty in teaching 69 pupils in the single room.' The following year saw a separate building erected a mile away from the schoolhouse and renamed the Union Institute which became in course of time the Union Institute Academy. The village of Trinity that grew up around the school was largely maintained by one industry, the boarding of students at the Academy. But no chances were taken with their morals as 'no people or houses of doubtful reputation were allowed within miles of the College.' Further, this was no public school on English lines; the College handbook - a 'catalogue' as it was known - stated 'This country affords no asylum for a learned Aristocracy and the people know far too little of profound learning, either to enjoy its advantages or reward its services', surely echoed in colonial government diktats in Africa ? Teacher training courses were taken together with the regular college course and so it became a Normal College, like the Ecoles Normales of France, but teacher training courses were discontinued after 1859 because of the low calibre of those leaving for the teaching field.

Therefore a reorganisation produced a three year B.A. course with emphasis on Latin, Greek, Mathematics and Natural Science, nowadays a somewhat archaic term distinguishing the usual science subjects from what was known as mental and moral science and the pure science of mathematics. But enthusiasm, as usual, was not enough without a solid foundation of excellent teaching to rescue the College from its reputation as a second rate institution, for it was an enthusiasm which had been diverted away from the needs and thought of modern life. Excessive emphasis on moral standards led to the College inducing the village shops to close when study hours began at night 'thus leaving no place for idlers of the town or country to congregate, and remove temptation from the student to be absent from his room at night' The governing body of the College was the North Carolina Conference of the Methodist Church which was satisfied that most of the students should become teachers and preachers.

34

The Civil War of 1861-65 halted all attempts at improvement. Senior students had been conscripted for the Confederate army and girls had been admitted to fill their places, until at last a shortage of provisions caused the college to close because more important was the feeding of the retreating army, chased by Sherman's forces. To a scene of chaos it reopened in 1866; formerly neat school buildings now resembled tobacco-barns, furniture and library books had been stolen and nobody at Trinity Village was prepared to board students. Although a long period of time, I shall pass over the next twenty years which was an era of slow recovery and reconstruction, a time when there was a greater emphasis on Natural Science, French and German, when the subject Greek was dropped, and, surprisingly, a course in Business Studies introduced in 1883 !

In the history of Trinity College the year 1887 might be regarded as the watershed of the institution. Firstly, the North Carolina Conference of Methodist Churches organised a fund to improve the finances of the College, raising a sum of 13,450 dollars of which the relatively small sum of $1,000 was donated by Washington Duke of Durham, North Carolina, an exceedingly successful tobacco manufacturer. It represented however, a signpost eventually directing Trinity College not only to Durham but to the status of a university. The same year proved remarkable in the appointment of John F. Crowell as President of Trinity College who organised and directed the transfer of the College from the isolated environment of Trinity to the more actively metropolitan venue of Durham in 1892. Crowell was an advocate of public schools - not in the English sense - supported by the state. He believed in studying the needs of the College community, both inside and outside its walls. A College board was formed whose members worked directly with the villagers on such problems as household sanitation in houses where students were boarded. His social philosophy is indicated in three quotes:

'Our national character needs to be disciplined and liberalised'

'Progress, involving a departure from the field of past experience to a new field of experiment, always requires a compromise among conflicting interests'

'To stagnate is to decline !'

Crowell broke with the tradition of the time in believing that the sexes should associate in various activities and thus students supported the Women's Christian Temperance Union and the Ladies Aid Society. They took part in what are described as merry social gatherings at picnics with the young women of the community, and although dances were not approved, occasionally a group of students, some dressed as women, held moonlight dances on the tennis court !

And lastly, though no doubt hardly noticed, Peter Nissen, aged 16, entered the preparatory section of the College. What formal education he had already received is unknown. Perhaps at a local primary school interspersed with mine visits whilst accompanying his father and practising the craft of the mining engineer ? Records which survive and are held by Duke University show that he attended preparatory, or secondary school, course in 1887-88 when the family lived at Thomasville, 12 miles west of Trinity. There is a gap of a year after which he attended the College proper in 1890-91 taking Freshman class (1st year) in at least English, and Sophomore classes in Chemistry and Political Economy for which we have the instructors' reports on their classes. Year long gaps in the continuity of their school careers were typical of many students having to work for their fees. During this period his home was at Albemarle, 40 miles south of Trinity. Again, I ponder on the passage of time on glancing at these reports of a century ago, 25 students in the English class, 22 for Political Economy and 21 in the Chemistry class, all with high marks suggesting some form of selective entry into the College by examination, and almost all had British surnames.

The average class marks have been calculated as follows, Nissen's marks in brackets, Political Economy 92 (92), Chemistry 86 (75), English 84 (92), but without reports on other subjects we can only conclude that in class he was an average student. Duke University archives assured me that when Peter Nissen was a student at Trinity College there were courses in civil and mining engineering, but Nora Chaffin's detailed volume, *Trinity College 1839-1892* lists civil and electrical engineering courses but there is no mention of mining. 'Average student' or not, there is evidence of a pleasant yet dynamic personality in as much as he was selected with others to be an assistant manager of the various functions which made up the week long Commencement Exercises of 1891, so-called because the graduates were about to commence their professional lives. The Annual Commencement

36

Exercise involved everyone in the College and the surrounding village of Trinity in a week long orgy of speeches and parties for staff and students, the presentation of degrees and medals, the latter for merit in various subjects. It was a public relations exercise ensuring for the following year not only the moral and financial support that had hitherto been enjoyed, but to strive for an increase in subscriptions to the North Carolina Conference of Methodist Churches which supported the College. Nowadays, degree presentations and prize givings are brief occasions and one might quail today at the prospect of a surfeit of addresses each evening for a whole week, especially as they were mostly of a serious and philosophical nature such as 'The Mystic symbolises the Real', 'All things bright must fade', 'Ever Onward', and 'Labour and the Reward', and although one could take a facetious line with all such addresses it appears that they were intended to be seriously moral. 'Things are not as they used to was' may have been a flippant reply to 'Plus ça change, plus c'est la même chose' but that was an exceptional title.

Trinity may have transferred to Durham N.C. in 1892 as a result of a further donation of $85,000 from Washington Duke but Peter Nissen was not among the students, having left in 1891 without completing the degree course in order to join the family for a second life in Nova Scotia. No reason is given for this change. Was there a further mining commission for Georg; or perhaps his wife, Annie, was homesick after an absence of 21 years ? Or, more likely, because brother Julius had obtained entrance to Dalhausie University, Halifax for the Chemistry course. What is known is that Peter Nissen attended for a short period a school of Art in New York, possibly to develop a natural talent for portrait sketching practised during church services with cartoons of congregation members ! But a strict upbringing at home and again at Trinity debarred him from joining the mainstream of Bohemian life as practised by his fellow students. Not only disappointed but shocked though not discouraged and declared that he preferred the company of simple unsophisticated miners ! The Nissens re-entered Nova Scotia with Georg now a United States citizen having in 1889 appeared at the Superior Court in Lexington N.C. as a 'mechanic' applying for citizenship, swearing to 'renounce allegiance and fidelity to every Foreign Prince, Potentate or Sovereignty whatever, particularly to Oscar 1st, King of Sweden and Norway', reminding us of the sovereignty of Sweden over Norway at that time. An inexplicable change, perhaps, for one about to live in a British Territory, but

TRINITY COLLEGE.   1-'91-Form 5-600

INSTRUCTOR'S REPORT

Of the _Sophomore_ Class in _Chemistry_ for the
Term ending _June 5 1891_ Date, _Jan 6_
Hours announced in Catalogue _63_   Time allowed _1 hr 30s._
Recitations actually Given _60_   Page of Catalogue ___

In the Freshman and Sophomore Classes *Monthly Examinations* are to be held in every study, and both examination and recitation grades reported on this blank.
In the Preparatory Department, weekly reviews and monthly examinations should be held in all the classes and be reported on this blank promptly.
All classes must have final examination just before Christmas recess and the summer vacation, unless arranged differently by consent of President.
Courses of instruction should be planned to end at Christmas, in time for examination.

NAMES.	RECIT. GRADE	EXAM. GRADE	AVERAGE.	TOTAL RECITATIONS ATTENDED.	REMARKS.
Barnes	92	95	93½	59	
Boggs	98	99	98½	59	
Burt	82	75	78½	60	
Baldwin	95	95	95	60	
Caviness	90	90	90	58	
Cahoon	85	85	85	60	
Cheatham	85	85	85	55	
Edwards	85	85	85	60	
Gattis	85	85	85	59	
Hearne	70	a	—		
Hester	70	fail	—	60	
James	95	95	95	60	Copied
Johnson	80	70	75	60	
Johnson	88	85	86½	60	
Merritt	88	82	81	58	
Nissen	80	75	77½	59	
Pete	84	75	79½	60	
Rowland	85	85	85	57	
Sasser	94	94	94	60	
Thompson	70	fail	—	58	
Turner	95	90	92½	59	

Signed, _W. H. Pegram_
INSTRUCTOR

The Chemistry Mark List for the Sophomore Class of 1890-91 at Trinity College, North Carolina.
(Courtesy of Duke University Archives, Durham, North Carolina)

Invitation to the Commencement Exercises of June 1891 at Trinity College. Nissen attended the college pictured on the Left-hand side. On the Right-hand side is the new Trinity College of 1892 built at Durham NC which Nissen did not attend. (Courtesy of Duke University Archives, Durham, North Carolina.)

James Halleck Crowell, Manager in Chief, Hall, Pennsylvania

ASSISTANT MANAGERS

F. B. Davis, N. C.
R. S. Davis, N. C.
W. W. Flowers, N. C.
L. T. Hartsell, N. C.

C. E. Turner, N. C.
P. N. Nissen, N. C.
W. T. Rowland, N. C.
F. C. McDowell, N. C.

Frank Armfield, Marshal in Chief, Monroe, North Carolina.

ASSISTANT MARSHALS

A. D. Barnes, N. C.
J. F. Hanes, N. C.
E. S. Green, N. C.
R. B. Crawford, N. C.

N. R. Reid, N. C.
H. R. Ihrie, N. C.
F. Winstead, N. C.
Howard James, N. C.

BACCALAUREATE SERMON
Rev. C. C. Woods, D.D., Missouri

LITERARY ADDRESS
Willie B. Dowd, Esq., North Carolina

MUSICAL DIRECTOR
Prof. R. J. Herndon, South Carolina

NOT *Waiting for Godot*. Perhaps Nissen's best effort in pen-and-ink. A conversation between a miner and, possibly, a tramp. (From the collection of P.C.M. Nissen.)

41

THE FALL OF THE DRILL SHED.

The Principal tenders Capt. Curtis his sympathies. "Never mind, we'll flood Convocation hall and the boys can have a good time yet this winter."

The semicircular shape of the Nissen Hut was derived from the Drill Shed roof at Queen's University, Kingston, Ontario. Nissen's cartoon was drawn when the roof collapsed under a heavy fall of snow. - This cartoon appears to have been published, but the source is unknown.
(From the collection of P.C.M. Nissen.)

42

XAMS.

Peter Nissen at Queen's University, Kingston, suggested a brain scan to find whether students have any ideas about English, Philosophy and Chemistry.
(Courtesy of Queen's University, Kingston, Ontario.)

A FOOTBALL GAME IN THE JUNGLE.

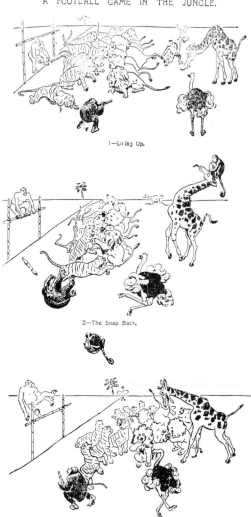

1—Lining Up.

2—The Snap Back.

3—The Goal.

In view of Nissen's quirky mind when at Queen's University, is it too fanciful to imagine that the animals represented certain students ?

(Courtesy of Queen's University, Kingston, Ontario. From the collection of P.C.M. Nissen.)

he was now 57 and may have intended to retire to the United States which he did in 1902.

In writing a biography of Peter Nissen it has been an immense disappointment in finding so little commentary and so few references to his life in Nova Scotia, Ontario and the United States from 1891 to 1910, after which the scene brightens considerably. But within those years there are a few incidents which, like individual fireworks blazing for several moments against a dark sky, enable us to trace vaguely his progress to a stage of resolute manhood which stood him well in the years beyond. Sadly, there was no Reid Jones at hand to give the detailed news which occupied pages of his letter about the family life at Thomasville. For the first time a residential address can be quoted, 148 South Street, Halifax, from the local Directory, and of the children only Julius is at home, Gurina is in Norway, and Peter is away but still in Halifax where he is employed in an engineering firm. Interest in Georg Nissen's ideas on stamp-mills suggested possible manufacture and to this end Peter Nissen was sent by the firm to the newly opened School of Mining sited in the grounds of Queen's University, Kingston, Ontario in 1896. 'Queen's' opened in 1841, sponsored like Trinity College, by a church but this one was Presbyterian so that the University had a distinct Scots atmosphere. Sited where the the St Lawrence river leaves Lake Ontario, Kingston was once a thriving ship-building port until the latter part of the 19th century when the local population turned gradually to agriculture and mining. In 1891 a 'School of Mining and Agriculture Fund' was established and subscriptions were invited. The fund became a Corporation under the Act respecting Benevolent, Provident and other Societies with capital stock of $100,000 divided into 1,000 shares of $100 each. The School was opened in October 1893 in a University building known then as the Science Hall, built for Chemistry and Physics, which was leased by the School from the University. The Departments of Chemistry and Mineralogy were taken over from the University resulting in degree subjects being taught to University students by the School of Mining staff, yet government funds for these subjects passed to the University. To attain this unethical situation the Chemistry and Mineralogy courses were advertised in the University Calendar and not in the School of Mining Calendar. The straitened finances of the School, especially in Engineering where one of the students reported; 'There is very little money for equipment.....We had a bench, an electric motor, one or two lathes and little else.' At first the government was unsympathetic, stating; 'The School of

Mining is looked upon by the government as a corporation distinct from the University and the government aids the Mining School as distinctively a Mining School'. It is unlikely that this situation would remain unknown to the government for long and so it decided as the result of a joint petition from both University and School that they should amalgamate, but it was not until 1916 that the relevant Act was passed by the Senate and the House of Commons of Canada. The designation, 'School of Mining and Agriculture' thus disappeared now that the whole complex was Queen's University, responsible to the government of Canada, and no longer the responsibility of the Presbyterian Church.

In certain respects the early history of 'Queen's' was a repeat of the Trinity College scenario where an educational institution is responsible to a church whose members favour the humanities rather than practical subjects, possibly placing emphasis on the production of teachers and ministers of religion. Whereas Trinity College resolved this situation speedily by curriculum changes because there was no technical school at hand, "Queen's", disposed of such students to the School of Mining. At "Queen's" the mining curricula included an unacceptable number of literary subjects such as English, French, German or Latin, Geometry, Algebra and Optics which gave the course what was then termed a 'university flavour' as distinct from a practical or professional character.

Yet whatever criticisms might have been levelled at the curricula, syllabuses and equipment, the staff recruited for the School of Mining had excellent qualifications and experience, among whom was William L. Goodwin, Professor of Chemistry, who had been a demonstrator to William Ramsay at University College, Bristol, the same Ramsey who with Rayleigh and Travers discovered the inert gases of the atmosphere, argon, neon, etc., whilst at University College, London. Professor William Nicol, responsible for mineralogy and assaying is remembered for his joking advice on mineral collections; 'If you ever see a good specimen in a private collection, try to get the owner to present it to the University. If he won't do this, try to buy it. If he won't sell it, steal it.' To him. a specimen in a private collection was wasted. Nobody can doubt that the Principal and his staff made heroic efforts to improve the technical image of the College by erecting a wood-frame building inappropriately named the 'Mechanical Laboratory' of which the main floor was the 'Machine Shop'. Students protested because it was intended to be their gymnasium and one night the wall of the Machine Shop was daubed with large letters displaying the ironic humour of the students, 'TOOL SHED' !

Then why did Peter Nissen enrol for the Mining Course ? It was little better than a junior technical school. We read, of course, that he was sent there by a Halifax engineering firm, but possibly there could be other reasons. His younger brother, Julius, was studying Chemistry at Dalhausie University in Halifax where William Mason was teaching Surveying and Mechanical Drawing until he left in 1893 to teach these subjects at the School of Mining at Kingston. There may have been some common interest between Nissen and Mason whilst in Halifax as Mason was also an artist, and further, it is recorded at 'Queen's' that Nissen attended Mason's course in Surveying I in 1896-97. Or was it merely the attraction of joining a new mining school ? The only other recorded fact is, 'In '96 or '97 Peter Nissen came to install a small stamp-mill.' There is a footnote, 'Inventor of the Nissen hut', but in the same volume there is never a reference to him as a student. The small stamp-mill was possibly one of the four mills constructed by Georg Nissen ? Lauretta Nissen sheds a ray of light on the subject when she writes;

'I do know from Peter himself that he worked as a Demonstrator on the Mining plant and....... earned his keep and studied geology at the same time.'

Professionally, 'Queen's' may have had little to offer Peter Nissen after a long practical experience with his father, but there were social activities to mould a man's character such as playing in an ice-hockey team, singing in the cathedral choir, sketching and ballroom dancing. Ice-hockey was played in the Drill Shed in winter when the floor was flooded and allowed to freeze. Nissen's cartoon, 'The fall of the Drill Shed' refers to an incident in the Winter of 1896 when a heavy fall of snow caused the roof to collapse. The Drill Shed had been bought from the Federal Government in 1880. In the cartoon the Principal, Dr George Grant, is commiserating with the ice-hockey Captain, and is saying; 'Never mind, we'll flood Convocational Hall and the boys can have a good time yet this Winter !' Perhaps Nissen is hoping for an alternative skating rink which was at hand in the form of a shed constructed in 1890 which was destroyed by fire in 1922. A very personal style of facetious inventiveness is expressed in the cartoons published in the Queen's University Journal of May 4th 1896 in which X-rays take the place of a normal

47

examination, classifying students according to whether their brain radiographs revealed the presence of 'ideas' about Chemistry, English and Philosophy. Did Nissen know of the dictionary definition, 'electromagnetic radiation..... able to pass through opaque bodies' ? In point of time it was an apt reference to the discovery of X-rays in the previous year (1895) by the German physicist William Konrad Röntgen. Nissen's 'professionalism' shows through by the inclusion of a vacuum tube and a transformer. We may be critical of the exaggerated distance of tube from film, but what does it matter? - the point of the cartoon is immediately clear. Barring ice-hockey, he was not interested in team games but we note the amusing symbolism expressed in a cartoon on American football, 'A Football Game in the Jungle' which was published in the *New York Journal.*

Nissen left the School of Mining without a degree in the subject which was awarded at the end of a three year course, the first of which began in 1895-96. His object was to continue prospecting in northern Ontario, where he had previously discovered a gold reef during a University vacation, and it is possible that he left before the course had finished to join Georg Nissen contracts until 1903 when Georg retired to southern California. What is lost is a wealth of information and adventure relating to contracts which Peter Nissen claims in every State of the United States and every Province of Canada ! Only a few surviving photographs tell us that from about 1900 to 1907 Nissen worked at Bunker Hill and Sullivan Mill at Kellogg, Idaho; The Boston Con Mill, Garfield, Utah; the Home Run Mill at Groom Creek, Arizona; at Bingham, Utah; and at El Tigre Mine, Mexico and not all of these can be located on a map. 'Lost' do I write ? Well ! not altogether. The story of Hornblende Mine is both a saga of technical success against natural odds and a romance.

When in later years Peter Nissen was applying for membership of the Savile Club in London, surprisingly, for it was patronised by literary folk, he described himself on the application form as 'Mining Engineer, Explorer and Artist', and if 'explorer' connotes 'discovery' then it is clear that the disappointingly unrecorded phase of Nissen's life in Ontario probably included the discovery of the Grace Mine which according to Lauretta Nissen occurred during a college vacation. Nissen would have easily recognised the difference between 'explorer' and 'prospector'. In snappy dictionary phrases there is little difference between these in terms but in practice, and in our mental vision, there is a whole spectrum of difference. Did Nissen sense that it was more tactful to describe himself in terms of one who might have received national and international acclaim, or heard in the halls of geographical societies, than to claim that he was one of the myriads of men, roughly dressed, wandering around the country chopping at rocks with a hammer. Both descriptions, of course, are caricatures but perhaps in applying for membership of a London club it was preferable to use a description implying 'status' and perhaps 'class', neither of which found a place in Nissen's vocabulary.

Travelling in a north-westerly direction from Kingston across the Province of Ontario we arrive at the coast of Lake Superior, opposite Michipicoton Island. A little inland is the town of Wawa where in 1896 an Indian found a gold-bearing lode which attracted a rush of prospectors of which one of them contracted Nissen to erect a stamp-mill. This was the Hornblende Mine, an almost impossible site, halfway down a cliff bordering on a lake. The difficulties in developing such a site are best illustrated by the photograph taken in 1926 when the mill-house had been converted into a residence for two prospectors. It housed a battery of two Nissen stamps which were found to work mechanically, but before any ore could be crushed and stamped the mining company was in liquidation. Disappointment was dispelled by a romance reminding me of young Lochinvar of Sir Walter Scott's poem. When at Queen's University he met Louisa Mair Richmond of Kingston, possibly on the dance floor rather than at the University. Peter Nissen excelled at ballroom dancing, and the Palais de Dance was the normal place to meet your future life-partner. They were to be married in Kingston on January 2nd 1900. Nissen was still working at Wawa, erecting stamp-mills on properties neighbouring the Hornblende Mine but gave himself time to travel the 470 miles to Kingston on snowshoes, assuming that the myriads of lakes en route were sufficiently frozen over for skating, but was accompanied by several Indians who could 'tell the ice'. All went well until they arrived at a lake where the ice was thawing, yet there was no alternative but to cross as a skating detour around the lake would dash all hopes of arriving at the church on time. The usual routine on such occasions was followed; rafts were constructed from fir branches which were carried whilst on safe ice and used when necessary by lying flat on a raft and working oneself forward. Thus he arrived in time and married his Louisa who was determined ever after to follow her Peter wherever he went - even to the mill-house at Wawa for the honeymoon ! But 470 miles ? Surely......?

Making comparisons between professional training today and that of our forbears may be unproductive unless there is a specific motive to justify such an enquiry. My motive is simple in theory if complicated in practice. How was it that a banal and bizarre education produced a mining engineer capable of putting into production an improved stamp-mill which would have been in use today but for the revolutionary changes in the mechanics of the gold-mining industry ? And by education I do not confine this enquiry to lessons and lectures at Trinity College and Queen's University but also to practical experience with Georg Nissen in a region almost the size of North America. It was to the great credit of two Trinity Presidents, Craven and Crowell, that they placed due emphasis on the importance of Natural Science, as it was known, in the College curriculum. Hampered as they were by a shortage of apparatus, they maintained a pressure for funds for this purpose. Crowell, especially, installed a biological laboratory enabling twelve students to carry out dissection although the types are not mentioned, perhaps frogs and rats ?

A chemical laboratory is mentioned and a museum containing, among other objects, minerals, rocks and fossils, many of which were presented by students and members of the public, encouraged by Crowell who in turn saw that the museum was open to the public as well as to the students. It was most fortunate that Nissen spent two years under this farsighted President whose presence induced the fresh wind of modernism to billow through an institution which tended to regard ancient learning too seriously. Yet one is a little sceptical and wonders whether the teaching of Engineering in Nissen's year at the College could possibly have been any more than a course in Applied Mathematics since the subject was taken by one who had previously taught Mathematics at Trinity for six years. I would have had greater confidence in the 'instructor in mathematics and electrical engineering' who was a graduate of the United States Naval Academy.

Before finally leaving Trinity, a pleasant story concerning the teacher of Civil Engineering in the year before Nissen's (1889-90) who also taught at various times History, Economics, International and Civil Law - a good all-rounder ? Crowell strongly came to the support of this man whose resignation was demanded by the North Carolina press because he spoke publicly of his belief that Democracy applied equally to Blacks as well as Whites !

In an age when mineral deposits can be located by space craft it might appear churlish in making a comparison between Nissen's education in Mining Engineering and the education available today. Also, Nissen's education might also be contrasted with the experiences and techniques of those who staked claims in California and the Klondike, washing river deposits in an iron pan or wooden batea. Apart from technical advances in the gold-mining industry it is worth considering the change in emphasis on several aspects of the industry. A leaflet on present day courses at a mining school lists a choice of seven out of ten courses in each of the three years required for a degree. It claims that the courses 'should be of interest if you are concerned about the utilisation of natural resources and *accompanying effects upon our environment.* (my italics); have an interest in the application of science and mathematics to large scale processes, and would like to understand materials, the methods and concepts of design with which industrialised society works.' Included in the courses are such subjects as communication skills, economics, management principles, industrial involvement and business studies. Part of the course can be spent abroad on vacation training and altogether the course is geared to the training of a professional engineer in a mineral related and environmental area.' Vacation employment reveals the variety of experiences available; 'A' spent his vacation in tungsten, china clay, coal and limestone mines and quarries. 'B' was in tin, bauxite (aluminium) and coal mines. Applicants are advised to spend a year in industry between school and university; the first woman to graduate at this mining school had previously worked at a gypsum mine, producing the raw material from which plaster of Paris is manufactured.

I might be accused of wandering from the theme of this biography but it highlights aspects of Nissen's mining education which differ from those of today. Training in an industrial subject today implies practical experience 'sandwiched' between college courses; in contrast, Nissen's limited college courses were 'sandwiched' between practical experience, perhaps not a disadvantage on a small mine where mine management has become a routine matter. Allied to this aspect is that Nissen and his father were one-metal miners, it was always gold. Was there ever a yearning for mining other minerals ?

The nature of 'sandwich' courses, and one-metal mining leads us to a third difference, present in today's mining but absent in an age that could forget the few woodlands and meadows lost to industrial development compared with the rural world that survived. It is doubtful whether the rape of the countryside was recognised in the gold-mines of North America as can be seen in old photographs which reveal the denudation of forests to provide fuel for steam engines which motivated the crushers and the stamp-mills. The modern emphasis on the protection, preservation and recovery of the environment is reflected in modern curricula of mining colleges. And, fourthly, the main challenge of starting and developing a mine nowadays is not in the technical production difficulties but in preparing a plausible and successful planning application which includes a blueprint for complete restoration of the site, once mining has ended. Yet in spite of such environmental regulation the dictates of governmental and local politics may override them. The tragic results of the United Kingdom government's demand for an increase of 66% in sand, gravel and rock over the next twenty years may involve the destruction of Thomas Hardy's 'Egdon Heath' for gravel, little Jack Horner's Mells (the 'Plum') for limestone, Croft Hill of the Druids for its granite and the countryside of the Norwich painters for its gravel, examples which, no doubt, can be repeated throughout the world. The Nissens had no such problems, working as they did in a continental vastness that then appeared impossible to ruin. The large scale scientific production of today and the mining world of the Nissens are decades apart and this should be understood in assessing the competency of Georg and Peter. Not for Peter Nissen the long full-time mining college which others enjoyed but a sporadic course attached firmly to a realistic practical experience at the mine; so bizarre, so strange, so exceptional, so singular it appears in today's world.

4. THE NISSEN STAMP MILL

Mention has been made in passing of the stamp-mill without plunging into technical details, but now an attempt must be made to describe its shape, locate its position at the mine and reveal its function. But first I shall mention the steps taken in separating gold from the rock, or ore, as practised by Nissen and his father at the beginning of this century. Underground, the gold-bearing rock was blasted with dynamite and roughly crushed. Trucks conveyed the roughly crushed rock to the shaft where it was hoisted to the surface and transported by conveyor belts to gyratory crushers each of which consisted of two rotary cones between which the ore was pulverised.

Conveyor belts then distributed the pulverised rock to the bins from whence it was delivered to the stamp-mills by sloping chutes. In the mills the pulverised rock was subjected to a continuous hammering by vertical steel stamps converting the pulverised rock to 'sand-pulp' - a 'pulp' because it is washed through the mill by water. Sand-pulp passed over copper plates coated with mercury that amalgamated with the gold. The gold amalgam was heated to obtain the gold, and the vaporised mercury was condensed to liquid mercury - a separation by distillation. Today the stamp-mill is replaced by the tube-mill; the mercury by sodium cyanide. This very brief account of gold extraction during the first two decades of this century is merely a background to the story of the stamp-mill which is the main interest, almost the whole interest, of this chapter.

The stamp had its origin in the mortar and pestle used by alchemists for the fine grinding of minerals, by apothecaries for the intimate mixing of drugs

53

A—Box laid flat on the ground.   B—Its bottom which is made of iron wire.
C—Box inverted.   D—Iron rods.   E—Box suspended from a beam, the inside
 being visible.   F—Box suspended from a beam, the outside being visible.

A Three-Stamp Mill of the 16th Century.
Broken rock is being wheeled to the stamp-mill, where it is partially crushed, followed by sieving
in a box, the bottom of which is made of wire netting. The 'Teeth' on the stamp stems connect
with the wide groove on the waterwheel shaft to produce a rise and fall of the stamps.
(The illustration is from *De Re Metallica* (about metals) by Georg Bauer (Agricola) 1555. Basle.
English translation 1912, 1912, Herbert C Hoover. Dover Publications Inc. New York.)

Two discarded five-stamp mills at the Rezende mine, Penhalonga, Rhodesia (Zimbabwe) which closed in 1955 when the reef worked out. As in a conventional mill, the stamps dropped into one long mortar, unlike the Nissen Stamp Mill where each stamp dropped into its own mortar.
(By kind permission of Johnson & Fletcher Ltd, Harare, from George Hindley, *Families in Partnership*, 1972, Mardon Printers, Harare - A history of Johnson & Fletcher, Ltd

and by artists in grinding coloured earths to fine powders. Larger pestles and mortars are used by African women for crushing maize to samp, with an accompanying working song. The stamp-mill evolved from the pestle and mortar at the beginning of the 16th century when the pestle, now activated by a water wheel, became a machine which crushed wet rock under iron-shod wooden stamps. That famous historian of early mining techniques, George Bauer of Saxony, writing under the name of Agricola, described in principle, in 1555, a one stamp mill powered by water, and used not for crushing ore but for breaking up slabs of copper from the foundry before refining them. In his book Agricola also illustrated mills of three or four stamps working on a flat unprotected surface, but some had mortar boxes in which rock was crushed without the loss of crushed ore.

Soon after his arrival in America in 1857, Georg Herman Nissen became critically interested in the Californian stamp-mill which he probably saw for the first time at Pike's Peak in the Rocky Mountains of Colorado in 1860. In the course of his varied mining experiences in Colorado, Nova Scotia and North Carolina, Georg diagnosed what he considered two important flaws in its design. First, he claimed that a heavier stamp would crush the ore more effectively - a fairly obvious conclusion provided safety checks were made on the framework of the mill. When Nissen stamps were eventually manufactured, their weight was 2,000 lbs, an advance on the 1,500 lbs of the Californian stamp. The second flaw was in the nature of the mortar which was long and rectangular into which dropped all five stamps of a battery. The ore passed from beneath one stamp to the next enabling some of the ore to escape uncrushed. Georg Nissen's recommendation was revolutionary ! Why not provide each stamp with its own circular mortar ? And then encircle each mortar with a metal screen allowing the finely crushed ore to be swept out by a stream of water, but holding back the coarsely crushed ore which is sucked towards the centre of the mortar in readiness for the next blow of the stamp. A secondary advantage was that the stamps beat evenly on their individual mortars, whereas the uneven pressure exerted by the stamps on the mortar of the Californian mill gave rise to a rocking motion no matter how firmly was the mortar fixed to its foundations. Further, a stamp needing a repair could be removed from the battery of stamps without stopping the action of the others, which was impossible with the Californian battery.

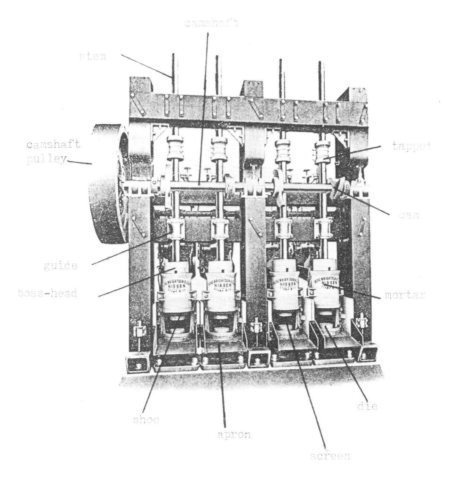

The Nissen 4-Stamp Mill: Ore from bins falls down the chutes to the mortar. Bins and chutes are hidden from view behind the stamps. The camshaft pulley is rotated by a belt attached to the engine. The rotating camshaft turns the cams by which each stamp is successively raised and lowered about 100 times per minute in crushing the ore on the die. The stream of running water sweeps the crushed ore, or sand-pulp, through a metal screen on to the copper 'apron' which directs the sand-pulp to the amalgamation tables. There the gold particles are separated from the sand-pulp by amalgamation with mercury.

(Illustration adapted from *"Nissen" Stamp Mills* 1924 ed. Head, Wrightson & Co Ltd. Stockton-on-Tees.

Courtesy of Davy International Ltd, Stockton-on-Tees. From the collection of P.C.M Nissen.)

Having satisfied himself that the existing stamp-mill could be bettered by the application of his ideas, he determined to build one. Already there has been an extract from Georg Nissen's memorandum belonging to Gurina; we continue here:-

"I left Nova Scotia for Upper Canada where I was engaged in mining until 1898. At that time I made the invention of my one-stamp mill which I had contemplated making for many years. I made four of these mills in Canada and I placed one in the Exhibition of Toronto, for which I was awarded a silver medal. I had every reason to believe that I was the first inventor of the one-stamp mill, at least, of one that was at all practical. I considered that if anyone had made such an invention they would have brought it before the public. I never saw a one stamp-mill or heard of one being built before I made my invention and I have studied stamp-mills ever since I began in 1860. I observed, that in a mortar where there are five stamps to a mortar, when the ore dropped in the mortar the stamp would fail to strike it, and would make several clips before the ore came in effectual contact with it. I considered that there ought to be some way by which to confine the ore so that it could not get beyond the reach of the stamp. Therefore, I invented this circular mortar because the enclosure had no corners, to which the ore could escape and therefore the stamp necessarily hits effectually when it descends. It has since proved that this stamp is perfect and that there is nothing to compare with it. Whoever has used this mill has been emphatic in saying that there is no room for improvement."

Full marks for enthusiasm and self-confidence but more than these were required to sell the stamp-mill as Peter Nissen came to realise. Of course, when Georg claims priority on invention he refers to each individual stamp mortar in a five stamp mill and not to the truly one stamp mill of the sixteenth century.

Nothing is known of Georg Nissen's mining in 'Upper Canada' except that he left Halifax, Nova Scotia, in about 1895 to settle at Toronto, leaving Peter Nissen at Kingston, to continue at the Hornblende Mine and at the Grace Mine nearby, which he is said to have discovered. This separation of father and son may have been precipitated by technical differences over the design of what became the Nissen Stamp Mill, according to Lauretta Nissen:

"I believe that at one time there was considerable friction between Peter and his father. Peter, it seems, made changes in the stamp and departed considerably from his father's original ideas. Georg was a masterful man, and did not relish having a son think he knew better than himself. I am glad to say that the feeling was short lived and vanished entirely."

It is doubtful whether the breach was short lived as we find that both were submitting to patent offices rival designs for the mortars of their mills. Pleasant memories of Wawa and the Hornblende Mine were insufficient to keep Peter Nissen there, now that the owners had become insolvent.

The hiatus between 'idea' and 'application' were proving too great a gap in time, even Georg's four mills, constructed in Toronto, could not resolve the application, for no account exists of how they fared under industrial conditions. One gained a silver medal at a Toronto exhibition and another installed in the School of Mining at Kingston. Peter Nissen appears to have realised that progress was only possible under two conditions; that he alone could develop Georg's ideas in a practical manner, and that a new field of operations, away from Ontario, was necessary. As far away as possible, it appears, to the south west of the United States, making his way to the goldfields of Arizona, settling first at Prescott, the former state capital. In the same year, 1904, he moved to Los Angeles where he was joined by his wife, Louisa, and baby daughter, Betty. A new field of operations demanded support from a company, which was established at Phoenix on November 15th of that year, known as the Nissen Engineering Company, with Nissen as President of the Board of Directors and brother Julius as Treasurer. Five other directors, possibly locals, completed the Board, but not Georg Herman Nissen.

Then followed the years of disappointment. Travelling from Arizona to Utah, thence to Idaho and even Mexico, selling the Nissen Stamp to new mines or inducing old ones to change. Sometime successful, but not always. Excitement when the first order was received in 1903 from the Home Run Mine at Groom Creek in Arizona, but despair when after a few years, the Nissen stamps were abandoned for the well tried Californian model, the manager having pronounced them a failure ! Joy when the stamps were bought by the El Tigre Mine in Mexico but there are no reports as to whether the mine continued working after the local tribe, the Orozquestos, attacked the mine in September 1912, looted the town and carried off $50,000 in gold and silver bullion. Again, vexation when the Bingham Mine in Utah

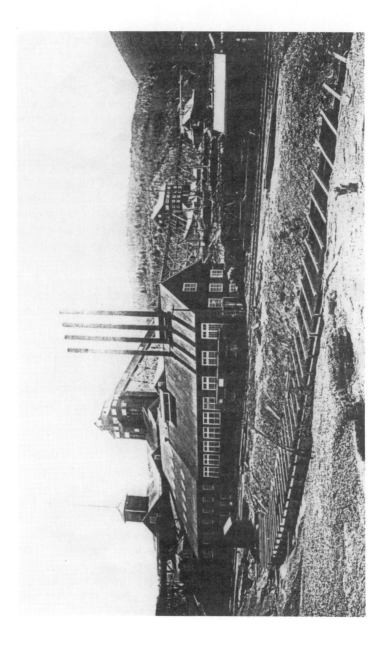

The Bunker Hill & Sullivan Mine, Kellogg, Idaho. 1907. During the first half of the twentieth century it was the largest lead mine in the United States. Peter Nissen was unable to market the Nissen Stamp Mill in Kellogg. (From the collection of P.C.M. Nissen.)

DATED 11th July 1910.

HEAD WRIGHTSON & CO.LTD

- and -

P. N. NISSEN ESQre.,

Copy

LICENCE to sell Nissens
Stamp Batteries under
Transvaal Patent.

Chamberlain & Co.,
1,Stone Buildings,
Lincolns Inn,
W.C.2.

The indenture Cover: A Nissen Stamp Battery contained four Stamps. Working alone, the Stamp Battery was also a Mill but the term "Nissen Stamp Mill" usually meant several Batteries, working together. (From the collection of P.C.M. Nissen.)

discontinued their use. Yet initially, 600 stamps had been sold in the United States and Canada. "Why is it now a failure ?" Peter Nissen must have asked himself, recognising that the theory of the Nissen stamp was indisputable. What was missing could be called the Triangle of Rapport between Inventor, Manufacturer and Mining Company, a liaison, requiring a Public Relations Officer, summed up in a letter to Lauretta Nissen in 1930 from Frank Stephenson who represented in South Africa the firm of Head Wrightson & Co, Ltd of Teesdale Ironworks, Cleveland. Said Stephenson:-

"The inventor of machinery is greatly at the mercy of the manufacturer. For one thing, really experienced manufacturers can nearly always improve the machines in all kinds of small practical ways and these make an immense difference. Also the firm must be rich enough and strong enough to push the machine in face of opposition from all rival manufacturers of similar machinery."

Nissen was already aware of these aspects of his problem which could be summed up in today's jargon as a lack of infrastructure in the mining industry of the United States, of which the Triangle of Rapport was one of the missing elements.

The crucial step was to disassociate himself, indeed, turn his back on the then weakly technological state of the United States and link up with a country more aware of modern mining methods. It was South Africa that called him, where for forty miles on either side of Johannesburg lay the mightiest reef of gold ore that the world had ever known - the Witwatersrand.

Years afterwards Nissen was heard to declare;
"I collected all the cash I could lay my hands on including a loan on my life insurance and took a passage for England for Louisa and Betty, who was about seven, and myself. I landed in England with only a few pounds in my pocket and the Patents and I had no friends or even introductions."

This was in 1910 when he was 39. In spite of having no contacts, he was soon discussing the stamp-mill project with the directors of Head, Wrightson and Co, Ltd of Teesdale Iron Works, Thornaby-on-Tees, Cleveland, a company formed in 1840 to manufacture cast iron window sashes for the new township of South Stockton. From this modest start it developed into a world-renowned manufacturer of cast iron, wrought iron and steel products which included wrought iron tunnel segments for the new London Underground and steelwork for Waterloo station. It was a highly successful firm until it closed in 1986 due to the recession and takeovers, a sad example of the United Kingdom's industrial decline. Meanwhile Peter, Louisa and Betty were living at Middleton One Row, a village between Thornaby and Darlington.

On the 11th day of July 1910 an Indenture was made between Head, Wrightson & Co, Ltd. and Peter Norman Nissen of 18 Upper Bedford Place, London. How extraordinary to note that apart from dates of birth, marriage and death, already found in a Norwegian family register, this is the first precise date recorded in our story so far ! The indenture, apart from an agreement on payments and royalties, revolves round the handling of the Transvaal Patent by which Nissen had secured patent rights within the Transvaal. We can assume that it became automatically a South African patent as the Union of South Africa had been proclaimed on the 31st of May 1910 uniting the former self-governing colonies of Transvaal, Natal, Orange Free State and the Cape of Good Hope. The Company agreed to pay 'the Inventor' the sum of £1,000 and 6% of the selling price of each stamp, but not on the first one hundred stamps sold. The Company could sell the stamps in all parts of the world except Australia, Canada, United States and Mexico where specific patents must have applied, linked to local manufacturers perhaps, such as those at Los Angeles and Toronto.   The inclusion of Australia is surprising. Nissen may have thought it wise to protect the invention in that country ? Or perhaps he once intended to migrate there as there was a viable gold mining industry which started with the first 'strike' at Bendigo in 1851 ? In the same Indenture, Nissen was appointed 'Engineer for Nissen Stamps' at a salary of £40 per month and transport expenses. Otherwise there were the usual guarantees that Nissen would be employed only by Head, Wrightson & Co, Ltd. and, whilst so employed, continually maintain the necessary payments to retain the Transvaal Patents for their advantage. With this hurdle behind him and the Inventor having found his Manufacturer, it was now the task to find a willing and innovative mining company, sufficiently skilled to test the stamp-mill, of the many that were taking advantage of the huge reef that lay at their feet.

Extreme climatic changes involving heat, frost, rain, wind and earthquakes loosed the gold-bearing ores of sub-Saharan Africa which were carried in flood and deposited in layers in a basin now known as the

The Mortar Box floor of two Nissen Stamp Mills at the Home Run Mine, Groom Creek, Yavapai County, Arizona, about 1903. In the foreground are the copper plates on which the gold is separated from the sand-pulp by amalgamating with mercury. The figure on the right is believed to be Peter Nissen.

(From the collection of P.C.M. Nissen.)

Witwatersrand, 'the ridge on either side of the white waters'. Traces of the original rock are to be found in Swaziland, Tanzania, Zimbabwe and Zaire, and it was these remnants that led prospectors astray and caused them to miss the main reef and to start mining at various peripheral locations in the northern Transvaal in 1873. Prospectors had found gold-bearing rocks but the reef eluded them, until from 1881 onwards the President of the Transvaal, Paul Kruger, insisted that concessions for mining be given to whole farms, which denied access to individual prospectors. These concession-holding entrepreneurs had the finance to purchase not only the farms but also the 'know-how' in the form of geologists and mining engineers. Not so the man who discovered the reef in 1886.

"My name is George Harrison and I came from newly discovered gold fields at Kliprivier especially from a farm owned by a certain Gert Oosthuizen. I have had long experience as an Australian gold digger and I think it is a payable gold-field."

This was one of the Langlaagte farms which was bought by Joseph Robinson who made 'millions', whilst Harrison lived modestly to the end of his days.

Meanwhile, the Nissens were living in Johannesburg, Betty was at school there, but the climate did not suit Louisa who was ill for most of the two years they spent there. Peter Nissen declared that next to England he would prefer to live in South Africa. In conversation with Lauretta:-
"He used to say that they found life inexpensive there though it is supposed to be expensive. They were very lucky in having a nice English cook who was a great comfort to Louisa in her illness. Peter was very fond of the black 'boys' and often talked about them, of their simplicity and good nature and how they learnt so quickly what they were shown and did it so neatly. He liked their clean white clothes and red ties and cheerful faces and used to laugh about how funny they looked if he happened to see them on their day out, dressed up in very bright and gaudy clothes and looking immensely pleased with themselves. He told how 'Charley' who was a specially nice and capable 'boy' came one day and said; "I go for holiday". Seeing their faces fall he hastily added, "I send cousin". Sure enough a new 'boy' soon appeared with Charley who showed him all he had to do, then he disappeared, to return when he had had a long enough holiday, a simplistic

65

but not unfriendly view of the African male, prevalent among European expatriates.

But to revert to the Stamp-mill and the fight for recognition, as he told it to Lauretta years afterwards:-

"I got the experimental plant going, and got excellent results, I published figures which proved that the stamp could do better than anything on the market, and, do you know, they would not believe my figures. They did not want to. They wouldn't come to see the plant ! I didn't know what to do, every week I expected a letter from Head, Wrightson to say I was not earning my salary. If the Stamp was not going to succeed here it would never succeed anywhere. There was a man called Bosqui, Consulting Engineer to the Rand Mines, he had great influence. Well, he would not come to see my results but he published a statement that my figures 'must be incorrect'. This was more than I could stand. I didn't care what happened, I went to his office and demanded to see him. "Look here Bosqui." I said "This won't do, you won't come and see for yourself and now you say I am a liar, it's not fair." Bosqui was so taken aback he said he would come, he came and was absolutely converted. He then generously published a refutation of all he had previously written against the Stamp. He said it was far ahead of any existing machinery. That turned the tide, from then the Stamp began to go.'

Nothing appears to be known of the circumstances under which a willing company was found, and found quickly, but it was the City Deep Ltd. which had been registered in 1899 on the farm Doornfontein in the south Witwatersrand. There had been previous occasions when this firm was willing to test suggested improvements in stamp battery designs and constructions. They agreed to manage a series of comparative tests with the Nissen mills and the Californian mills, conducted and financed by the Central Mining and Investment Corporation, presumably a neutral body. Both mills were run by the same millman, an unusually skilled worker whose name, unfortunately, is not recorded but perhaps the most important member of the testing group. Two independent referees were engaged by the Company, F.L. Bosqui, Consultant Metallurgist - yes ! the very same and erstwhile doubting Bosqui, and J.H. Rider, Consulting Electrical and Mechanical Engineer. It was now Nissen, the engineer, quietly using scientific method to prove the superiority of his Stamp, before Nissen the salesman could emerge. A more unobtrusive entry by a salesman could hardly be imagined. At the December 16th meeting of the Chemical, Metallurgical and Mining Society of South Africa one member recognised his modesty, unusual in that country;

"These people brought their stamp into our midst quite quietly and with no beating of the big drum !" And continued "No problem. no shouting, no jaw-tons' of expended energy." I especially like the unit of vocal energy - the jaw-ton.

Before a comparison on the industrial scale could be made between the two stamps, the Nissen and the Californian, it was necessary to discover how much crushed dry ore could be stamped in 24 hours by each stamp working in a Nissen four stamp unit and in a ten stamp Californian unit. Nissen refers to the latter as a 'City Deep' unit. Five pilot tests were made from June 23rd to September 16th, 1911 and the average results of the crushing were;-

	Nissen	City Deep
Dry ore crushed - tons	185	196
Total run (hours)	36	22
Tons per stamp per 24 hours	31	21

(or the 'DUTY')

Each battery was supplied with about 200 tons of ore. The Nissen battery was crushing for 36 hours whilst the City Deep battery, with a greater number of stamps, required only 22 hours. However, the Nissen stamp demonstrated its superiority in crushing 31 tons in 24 hours as compared with the City Deep output of 21 tons. The essential facts were now available to establish an experimental programme not for just two batteries but for a mill-size comparison involving a month's crushing of 40,000 tons of ore or 1,333 tons per 24 hours, therefore the number of stamps required for the tests were calculated thus:

Nissen	$1333/31 = 43$ i.e., 6 batteries of 8 stamps $= 48$
City Deep	$1333/21 = 63$ i.e., 7 batteries of 10 stamps $= 70$

As Nissen coupled two of his units of 4 stamps he required a multiple of 8 stamps i.e., 48 stamps made up of 6 batteries. The City Deep Mill required 70 stamps composed of 7 batteries of 10 stamps each. Then why did Nissen assemble 100 City Deep stamps when 70 would have been sufficient ? An arithmetical error perhaps, as he used the value of 14.8, or nearly 15 as the City Deep duty instead of 21 which meant that his calculation of the number of stamps required for the tests was 1333/15 or 89, taking the number of stamps as 100 for a certain match ? This discovery sent me post-haste to a London library to re-read the original journals of 1911 and 1912. There, in the Institute of Mining and Metallurgy, I found a partial answer to this contradiction of experimental results, especially as the tests on both mills were intended to produce the same tonnage of crushed ore in the same time.

Theoretically, Nissen was justified in using 100 City Deep stamps each with a duty of 15 tons per 24 hours, and if 70 stamps had been used the City Deep mill would not have finished crushing at the end of each 24 hour period, a happening which would have been noticed by the millman and Nissen. My conclusion is that the Duty of the City Deep stamps varied considerably, but during the monthly test and the daily test, the average Duty was actually about 15 tons per 24 hours. However, whether 100 stamps or 70 were used in the City Deep mill, the test results showed that the Nissen mill was not only superior to the City Deep mill in crushing power but also superior in other ways such as power consumption and cost and the wear on shoes which crushed the ore, and the wear on the dies on which the ore was crushed.

A formidable opponent and critic of Nissen's calculations was Mr A.M. Kratz who, by another arithmetical route, had concluded that only 70 City Deep stamps were necessary for the tests. A clever man - he had twisted the concept of 'duty' into a term which expressed the relationship between 'tons of ore crushed per 24 hours' and 'length of mill', claiming that length of mill involved capital cost, the power cost and cost of pumping water to mortars, and thought he had proved the superiority of the City Deep stamp over Nissen's. However, he had miscalculated the length of Nissen's mill by ignoring the fact that Nissen had not used separate four stamp batteries but had combined them in pairs, thus reducing the length of his mill. 'Duty' according to production of crushed ore was a realistic concept, which invalidated Kratz's criticism. But Kratz must be given credit for a research which further highlighted Nissen's claim to have produced a superior stamp.

The City Deep millman had suggested that an increase in stem length would improve the duty of his stamps, but Kratz, from careful drawings of both stamps, showed that this would mean a high centre of gravity with consequent increased vibration, which was confirmed in practice when vibration at the guides was more noticeable with the resultant guide friction. Therefore the lower gravity of the heavier Nissen stamps further justified their claim to be superior to the conventional stamps.

If I am to avoid turning this biography into a technical guide-book there should be reference to the polemical discussions which seemingly had the atmosphere of theatre and drama therein as today the cold print shouts from the pages of the Society's Journal. As Lauretta Nissen neatly puts it;
"...so if we choose we can still hear the echoes of the struggle which meant so much to Peter." He had his supporters, of course, those who felt that the conventional (Californian) stamp mill needed updating and improving yet a fresh start was imperative in a technological area which had stagnated, said one member.
"...and the only fault I have to find is that Mr Nissen did not come here years ago !"

Who were his opponents ? There were those who regarded changes as anathema, who pleaded for improvements in the Californian stamp mill, when for decades there had appeared no fundamental design change, merely material changes in the manufacture of components when they failed the strenuous work conditions of the mill. One must remember also that there had been huge capital investment in Californian stamps across Witwatersrand and a substitute would not only have to be better, but superlatively better. Some mines were well equipped but there were others where crushed ore travelled by conveyor belts, watched by lines of Africans who retrieved the large uncrushed waste rock, dropping it through pipes in the floor to be collected for use in the tube mill where by impact and abrasion they ground crushed ore from the stamp mills to a fine powder. The tube mill was still a newcomer to the Witwatersrand scene. The year saw George and Henry Denny experimenting with a new crushing process by which roughly pulverised rock was reduced to pulp in a rapidly rotating steel cylinder containing, at first, pieces of hard rock, and later steel balls. The Dennys were consulting engineers to the General Mining and Finance Corporation in Johannesburg and it was in 1904 that the tube mills were beginning to be installed on the

Witwatersrand. Dependency upon lowly paid untutored labour has prevented the rapid advance of invention in Africa, and although this was not hinted overtly, it could possibly have been an aspect of opposition to change.

Others, including Lashinger, the vice-president of the Society, questioned the validity of Nissen's figures, and other 'smear' tactics were to accuse him of 'incorrect claims based on incorrect statements and also unfair comparisons with existing mills.' Perhaps a plausible criticism is Nissen's faith in the superiority of any gravity stamp mill over other means of ore crushing, little realising that the role of the future improved tube mill would oust the stamp as an agent of fine grinding. He had always expressed great admiration for the 'workaholic' Californian stamp mill. Was it, perhaps, a 'cosy' sound of stamps, especially at night at a distance which may have enamoured him as it did me when living in Bulawayo in 1934, listening to the chattering of surrounding small workings, when old residents could point to the sound and name the mines, one after another ? Yet the Society owed it to Kratz, who predicted the future when all half inch ore from the preliminary crushers would pass directly to the tube mills rendering the stamp mill obsolete, but a World War was to intervene before the tube mill became paramount.

To return to Nissen's lecture and the discussion that followed. It was probably the greatest 'in-depth' examination, not only of the Nissen stamp but of stamps in general. The emphasis was mainly on 'stamps' rather than on 'mills' or 'batteries' of stamps, as it was generally acknowledged that the Nissen unit was more productive than the Californian of similar ore-crushing capacity. When on October 21st 1911, Nissen started the debate with his classic lecture 'Notes on High Duty Gravity Stamp Mills', on fourteen quarto pages, he was speaking as a newly elected member of the Chemical Metallurgical and Mining Society of South Africa, who was wasting no time in making his 'maiden speech' to an audience of 85 from the then modest town of Johannesburg. Discussion followed and was continued at the Society's monthly meetings in November 1911, December 1911, and January 1912, and finally, on March 16th 1912, when the meeting was almost fully devoted to Nissen's 'Reply to Discussion'. Such generous time allowed to a new member, suggests that his paper was given an encouraging reception and a complete reading of the discussions confirms this view. It is, therefore, difficult to understand why Nissen, in conversation with Lauretta, gave such a hostile view of the debate with accusations targeted at the vice-president of the

70

Society, who took objection to Nissen's claim that the lower ore bins, which supplied the stamps via the chutes, meant a financial saving on mill structure. Later experience at the mines showed that Lashinger was right when it was found necessary to raise the chutes to give a steeper angle down which the ore could slide without causing a blockage, removable only by African labour ! Yet Lashinger was pushing scientific method too far when he doubted the accuracy of Nissen's limited experimental results which could be ultimately confirmed only after a longer series of trials, which would have corroborated Lashinger's own statement, one of the most significant of the debate, that 'Conditions of the feed have probably more to do with the efficiency of the stamp than any other factor connected with it.'

The feeling of the meeting warmed considerably towards Nissen as it learnt of his methods of establishing the facts and even his arch-critic Lashinger admitted that he 'deserves encouragement and recognition of his effort when working in a field peculiarly beset with difficulties and hedged about with discouragements." His other critic, Kratz, conceded that; "Mr Nissen's paper is an exceptionally good one"......and of the Nissen unit; "A beautifully compact unit and will make its way." From a Mr R.A. Barry; "...We must, I think, all agree that the Nissen method of putting things before us is one that could be adopted far more widely that ever it has been in the past..." Apart from its superior crushing reputation it had been demonstrated that there was a saving in power from 0.8 pence to 1.0 pence per ton of ore milled, a reduced maintenance expenditure, and a reduced capital expenditure. So ended what must have been one of the most remarkable debates in mining history, the record of which appears to deserve greater publicity.

For the remainder of his two years with Head, Wrightson & Co, Ltd. his sales record was a success, if sporadic, as shown by the distribution of stamps among several mines, some buying two stamps only, whilst others accounted for 56. The City Deep Ltd, where Nissen demonstrated the superiority of his stamp, appears to have used only four Nissen stamps. Whilst during the period 1914-1922 the number of Californian stamps rose from 190 to 350, this increase could be accounted for by the acquisition of five other mines and their plant. Sales were made in the Transvaal, Southern Rhodesia (Now Zimbabwe), Cornwall, Russia, Sardinia, Argentina, India, Egypt 'and many others' according to the 1924 catalogue of Head, Wrightson & Co, Ltd. The main sales may have ceased by 1924 as in the Transvaal there were no large scale installations of stamp mills after 1918. In the same catalogue the manufacturers claim that they have sold 300 Nissen stamps 'in different parts of the world !' Whatever the number, the firm was very satisfied with Nissen's salesmanship - "The best salesman he ever met, because he believed so implicitly in the thing he tried to sell." A valued testimonial from one of the directors.

Essential 'After-sales' service appears, not only in the receipts sent periodically to Nissen, but in the reports of Frank Stephenson, already mentioned in this chapter. He was the Southern Africa representative of Head, Wrightson & Co, Ltd. based in Johannesburg, but often travelling to the mines which were the Company's customers. This was no social round as can be gathered from his reports, but a detailed series of discussions with mine managers that spoke of working difficulties, wear and tear of machinery and breakages, although skilled engineers and well equipped workshops maintained almost continuous working at the mills. Breakages were not a surprising item when one knows that the 2,000 lb gravity stamps drop on the rock about 100 times a minute, through a distance of eight inches for 24 hours! I was especially interested in an October 1918 report of a visit to the Bushtick Mine in Southern Rhodesia, near the present Mzingwane Secondary School, where I was headmaster from 1960 to 1966. The mine has closed but the site is occupied by an independent secondary school and a lime works. The 24 hour tests at the City Deep mine, already mentioned, failed to anticipate in such a short time the difficulties arising over a longer period. The chutes, down which passed the rock to the stamps, fuelled a general complaint. Each supplied a mortar and was actuated by a rope raised and lowered by the up and down movement of a tappet, which in turn, was moved by a cam on a camshaft, and so - 'The feeder chute is set at too small an angle: feeders had to be raised to get the rock to slide down into the mortar.' Again, at the Kimberley Reef mine in the Transvaal, "Two feeders out of action, boys hand feeding down chute. Feeders choke with extra coarse feed and boys required to constantly clear." Manual feeding by 'boys' (adults, really.) prevented the shutting down of the stamp. The Kimberley Reef report makes depressing reading, damaged mortars, broken stem guides, alleged unsatisfactory design and material, but Frank Stephenson finishes his report with; "The Kimberley Reef Battery has undoubtedly been ill used and neglected....." Which explains much. But better news from the Bushtick

Mine;- "As I previously reported, Mr Burnett (The Mine Manager) is distinctly pleased with the Nissen stamp as a crushing medium and would undoubtedly install more stamps of this type, if extensions were decided upon. He would,, however,draw up his own specification and include such modifications as he considered necessary....."

Sales of stamps were, at first, encouraging but after the 1914 -1918 war the demand ended in 1926. The tube mill, backed by improved gyratory crushers, was becoming a grinder of increasing importance. The year 1904 first saw it on the Witwatersrand as a fine grinder following the crushing by the stamp-mill, but the newly high powered gyratory crushers eliminated the need for stamp mills which had outlasted their usefulness. However, by 1934 there were still some 5600 stamps on the Witwatersrand of which 88 were Nissen stamps in use in 31 mines, but on the other seven mines, all new, no stamp-mills had been installed. Peter Nissen had moved into an era of rapidly evolving industry in which he was, to a certain extent, initially responsible. The invention of the Nissen stamp-mill had raised various economic and technical questions which had been partially answered by others in the invention of the gyratory crusher and the tube-mill and their application to the flow sheet of the gold extraction industry.

Who then, invented the Nissen stamp-mill ? Georg ? Peter ? or both ? With a certain dogged, but characteristic foresight Georg had written at his daughter, Gurina's request;-
"At that time (1898) I made the invention of my one-stamp mill, which I had contemplated making for many years.... I had every reason to believe that I was the first inventor of the one stamp-mill."
Georg Nissen first asserted his claim in a practical manner when mortars of the Hornblende mine in Ontario were moulded,

G H Nissen
Toronto
Pat. Applied for

That was about 1899 when he was living in Toronto. The Application was filed in January 1990 with the United States Patent Office in Washington but was not registered until July 1907. Possibly, Georg was visiting Norway

73

when Peter Nissen installed a stamp-mill in about 1903 at the Home Run Mine at Groom Creek, Yakapui County, Arizona. On the moulding reads;-

Nissen's system
Manf'd
Llewellyn
Iron Works
L.A. Cal.

which leaves us guessing - Which Nissen ?

Meanwhile Peter Nissen had forwarded to the US patent Office two patent applications, the first, dated February 1904 and registered in November of the same year. It was similar to Georg's Application of January 1900, but I can only assume that it was accepted because it contained some improvements in the mortar, such as a port or hole through which a hand could be inserted to remove foreign matter which might obstruct the screen through which the finely crushed 'sand pulp' passed. Peter Nissen followed this patent with another in September 1904, patented in December 1910, in which the mortar was constructed of removable parts so that a broken member could be removed and replaced by another. Therefore, contrary to the usual statements in obituaries and *Who was Who*, I conclude that the Nissen Stamp Mill was 'invented' by Georg Hermann Nissen and that he had priority of patent. Or am I using an obsolete language form which fails to recognise that the term 'inventor' applies to an unknown 16th century miner in Saxony who first coupled together three stamps powered by water energy ? Further, that he was followed by 'innovators' who, in turn, introduced the conventional mortar of the Californian stamp mill, then Georg Nissen with his concept of a separate mortar for each stamp, and finally, Peter Nissen with his system of replaceable parts, all of which I shall discuss in the final chapter, 'Nissen - Man and Inventor ?'

Not only did Georg Nissen claim that he invented the Nissen Stamp Mill, but stated confidently that; "Whoever has used this mill has been emphatic in saying that there is no room for improvement." How right he was ! But, did he appreciate that the Nissens had taken the machine to the end of a stamp-mill cul-de-sac ? Or that another avenue could be found - if not already found ? I doubt it ! The progress of science, and engineering too, I should imagine, is

74

not continuous; candles followed by paraffin, then gas, then electricity, disparate means of illumination. An expanding parameter comes to a halt and disappears into the history of science to be followed later by another expanding parameter of discovery. But within an existing parameter there are discoveries and their applications - first the idea - then the application. Two ideas which distanced the Nissen stamp mill from the others was the individual mortar for each stamp and the heavier stamp. But Georg Nissen's presentation was, perhaps, faulty and the cause of the delayed acceptance of the mill was also due to a lack of testing. It was left to Peter Nissen to organise and supervise the 'running in' period at the City Deep mine, which the ideas so badly needed before they became workable and reliable. The ideas can be attributed to Georg Nissen, but the successful, if short, history of the Nissen stamp mill was due to the experimental management and public relationship skills of Peter Nissen. Not only was it a classic experiment in the history of mining, but in a more important aspect a chapter in the history of ideas.

Back in an England at war with Germany since 4th August 1914. In a letter of 4th November 1914 to Head, Wrightson & Co, Ltd, from their South African representative, Frank Stephenson:-

"Dear Sirs,

I returned to Johannesburg from my visit to Rhodesia on 25th ulto having been away for four weeks. The trouble in Europe, German South West Africa and the Union of South Africa has considerably affected all classes and in the present unsettled state, the war appeared to be the only matter discussed. In addition to this the continued drought has seriously handicapped the mines, many of which are closed down...."

And to confirm the last sentence, an item from the July-August account of the Shamva mine in Rhodesia;-

'Water per 1,000 galls 4.00 pence. Pumping for 8 miles.'

Meanwhile, Nissen, six thousand miles away from the difficult circumstances of Southern African mining, was trying, in vain, to join the British army, but rejected because of his age - 43 - even by the Royal Engineers !

"Who do you know ?" At last, January 19th, 1915, through the good offices of a friend, he became a temporary lieutenant in the 12th Battalion of the Sherwood Foresters, an infantry regiment.

"What do you know ?" Agonising over a platoon shifting timber in a chaotic fashion he demonstrated a better method in what is known as a 'time and motion study', which so impressed a passing officer who asked;

"Surely, you must be an engineer !"

"Of course, I'm an engineer, but it doesn't seem to matter in this bloody war !" replied Nissen.

A few days later, the officer having mentioned the incident to the local headquarters of the Royal Engineers, Nissen was transferred to the 103rd Field Company Royal Engineers in May 1915 and left with them for France in August, spending the first night under a tree near Hesdin in the Pas-de-Calais. His movements are unknown until the beginning of 1916 when he was stationed at Ypres in what was probably the bloodiest year in the history of war. Verdun was besieged from February to December and to relieve the German pressure a French and British offensive was planned for July. Obvious though it was to many, there appeared to be several senior officers claiming, rather peevishly, that they had made the suggestion originally that accommodation, or 'hutting' was necessary because the French villages in the area had been destroyed by gunfire and, therefore, it was impossible to billet soldiers in them. Nissen, who was at Ypres, had foreseen this problem and was already sketching curious looking semi-circular huts - floor and roof, but no walls - not the off-duty fantasies of a temporary lieutenant, but the genesis of the Nissen hut.

5. FROM SKATING RINK TO NISSEN HUT

Indeed ! It started from memories of the skating rink at Queen's University, Kingston, Ontario and referred to by Lauretta Nissen in her typed notes:-

"Peter used to tell of his invention of the hut. He knew how badly hutting was needed and said; "I was lying in bed, thinking intensely," as was his habit when a problem occupied his mind, "about huts when, suddenly I thought of making it semicircular. I lay and thought and it all seemed to come quite clearly, then I got up and found a pencil and made a rough sketch and then I went to sleep." In 1920, Nissen, when at Kingston, addressed a crowded meeting of the Engineering Society of Queen's University. In the course of his speech he described how, in 1916, he had realised the need for a standard hut for troops. He told his hearers that while working out the problem of a possible hut in his mind, he recalled the Kingston Skating Rink in the Drill Shed at Queen's and said that was the real father of the Nissen Hut.

Curiously enough, continues Lauretta:-

"Among the little cartoons drawn by Peter, which happened to be preserved from The *Queen's Journal,* is one called 'The Fall of the Drill Shed'. Principal Grant, in cap and gown is talking to 'Captain Curtis', who appears in skates, holding a hockey stick. Behind the two figures are the ruins of a semicircular 1880 building much like a large Nissen hut. Evidently, the Rink, Peter had in mind." Lauretta Nissen was mistaken in thinking that this cartoon, like others, was published, but it was found among family papers and already seen in Chapter 3.

77

Semi-circular buildings of 1890. In the background is the first covered ice-hockey rink in Ontario, at Queen's University, Kingston, Ontario. (Courtesy of Mr Paul Banfield, Archivist at the University.)

ERECTING A NISSEN HUT.

These photographs are of 'mock-ups' which illustrate stages in the erection of a Nissen hut. The jointing of the horizontal wooden purlins to the steel ribs, or bows, is not shown but this is explained in a later sketch - (The Hook Bolt.)

Above. Wooden bearers are laid on level ground.
Below. Steel ribs are bolted to the bearers and wooden purlins fixed to the ribs with hook-bolts

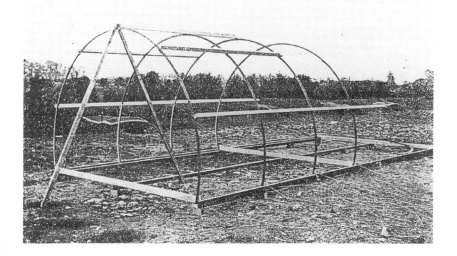

Above. Wooden joists are screwed to the bearers. These joists support the wooden floor panels.
Below. The inner lining of light corrugated iron, with horizontal corrugations, is fixed behind the 'T' of each rib. The outside sheets, with vertical corrugations, are then fixed over the inner lining. The ends of the hut are covered with vertical boarding with battens over the joints.
(From *Instructions for erecting 16ft Span Nissen Huts*, Nissen Buildings Ltd, Rye house, Hoddesdon, Herts.

(All four photographs are courtesy of Schreiber Furniture Ltd.)

A certain journalistic effort has given rise to a fanciful story of how Nissen, awakened from sleep at Ypres in Belgium, conceived the plan of a hut, arose and drafted a sketch inspired by the memories of the Drill Shed after which he immediately constructed a hut from whatever metal sheets were available, aided by a bending machine borrowed from a Canadian regiment ! A suitable scenario for a television feature, but too telescoped to be plausible. The approach to an ideal hut was a more casual proceeding, involving the building of several huts in succession, to be inspected by various members of the Royal Engineers hierarchy, many anxious that their suggestions for improvement should be noted. Possibly because a Royal Engineers building was often given an eponymous title, such as the 'Romney', the 'Laing', the 'Liddell', and the 'Armstrong' hut, after names of R.E. personnel. Was it to be a 'Nissen' hut ? But firstly, who suggested the need for huts, or 'hutting', to use the army term and, secondly, who suggested the form of the hut that was finally accepted ? Between Nissen, now a major, and his Commanding Officer at Montreuil, Lieut Colonel Bertram Shelley, there was a gradually escalating difference of opinion, as to who first advised the use of hutting. Shelley claiming that it was he who mentioned the subject to Nissen when about to return to the United Kingdom on home leave, about the middle of April 1916, but Nissen insisted that the subject was not broached until Shelley had returned from leave at the end of April, to find that Nissen had already constructed a possible prototype. However, Shelley admitted that he was uncertain whether he had advocated hutting before proceeding on leave, but after the war had ceased, about seven years after, Lauretta Nissen made a record of her husband's account:-

"Whilst still at Ypres, I introduced my scheme to General Capper, who wrote to General Plumer who in turn took up the matter and introduced me to the Engineer-in- Chief as 'too valuable an inventor for a Field Company R.E.' So I was transferred to General Headquarters 2. On 16th March 1916 I went to 29th Company R.E. General Headquarters, under command of Colonel Shelley."

It was General Capper who, in September of the previous year, was involved in a personal strategy which saved hundreds of infantry lives in the bloody and unwanted battle of Loos. Instead of sending in reserve troops behind an already annihilated brigade on his left, he directed them, successfully, to his right where another brigade had effected a breakthough against enemy fire.

The Deputy Engineer-in-Chief was Brigadier General William Andre Liddell, who was no office-closeted soldier, but had his ear to the ground. He was aware, not only of these claims and counter-claims, but also that no minutes had been recorded at various meetings about the hut. He wrote to the various officers concerned, asking them to recall their memories of what was decided at those meetings. Hardly a wartime assignment to write the history of war in the midst of battle and it was not surprising that Liddell's exercise was not completed until April 1918, after a lapse of two years. Yet priorities were established and credit was given where deserved.

Here is Liddell:-

16.4.18

To Lieut Col Shelley,

1. "I started this question because I thought it would be interesting to have on record a statement of various officers' share in the design which has proved so successful and on which 2½ million pounds will have eventually been expended.

2. The main idea of a semicircular pattern of hut on which all the rest depends is entirely Major Nissen's. The design of fittings is also (his) to a great extent. By far the greatest share of credit of the successful supply of huts is due to Major Nissen, who possesses knowledge of workshop practice which the other officers concerned lack.

3. Consequently, the hut has been known by his name and he has been allowed to patent the design. I think that all the Officers named in the notes, Lt Col Shelley, more than any other, Lt Col Sewell and Lt Col MacDonald have, by reason of their knowledge of military requirements and of material available and their wide experience contributed to a great extent in making the design practical and satisfactory, by introducing the improvements attributed to them."

W.A. Liddell
Deputy Engineer in Chief

This endorsement of Nissen's claim to be the inventor was essential, as we shall see, in the post-war years. Meanwhile, like a casual reader anxious to know nothing more than the beginning and end of a story, I must now mention the events which connect them, in a mini saga of adjustments and alterations essential for urgent ordering of eventually 100,000 huts from

Nissen at Hesdin, Pas de Calais, France, where prototype huts were designed and constructed before plans were sent to the United Kingdom for the manufacturing of the hut parts.
(From the collection of P.C.M. Nissen.)

factories in the United Kingdom. The facts are embedded in correspondence between Lt Col Shelley, Major Nissen and Gen Liddell.

First, Shelley to Liddell:- 11.4.17

"While at St Omer, I realised that there was a demand for a portable hut, and that nothing I had seen fulfilled requirements. Attempts to solve the problem were being made, but had to be suspended owing to the pressure of work entailed through the transfer of General Headquarters to its present site. Towards the middle of April 1916, work had slackened somewhat and as labour became available, I suggested to Major Nissen that he should take up the question. This was just before I went on leave. On my return after Easter, I found he had started on the construction of a semi-circular hut. At that stage it consisted of a couple of bays with wooden bows, and a floor at one end. The bows were made of 3/4" rough boarding bent to a curve and then nailed together. They were made in three sections and covered with curved corrugated sheets held to purlins by iron straps. The end was of plain boarding, nailed to studding, like weather boarding and there was no lining. I pointed out to Major Nissen that a lining was essential and suggested a way of fixing without nailing, but he improved upon this by grooving the bows. The method of fixing the sheets was unsatisfactory and hook bolts were used in lieu. The hut was completed and measured 18' x 18'. It was made in three bays. (It) had a window in each side and two small windows and a door at each end. The lining was 5/8" rebated boarding and 5 sheets of corrugated iron were used to the ring. (He refers to the semicircular bow.) You inspected the hut, considered it was too high and I think at the same time the thickness of the lining was reduced.

A second hut was built, 20' long by 18' wide, but generally similar to No 1. A second conference took place with Lt Col B H Armstrong from the War Office being present. The wooden bows were not considered satisfactory and Major Nissen suggested using iron ribs. The question of rolling special sections was discussed but eventually Major Nissen evolved the present method of holding the lining in place. At your suggestion the size of the hut was further modified to its present dimensions of 27' x 16', side windows were omitted and standard doors and windows introduced.

The third hut was then built. Matchboarding was introduced in place of rebated boards. I altered the panelling at the ends, doing away with the cross transom and re-arranging the studding to very much as now adopted.

The ends were covered with 2 ply panels similar to the Tarrant Hut. The hut proved a success, but several minor alterations were introduced. Parts were simplified, at your suggestion and each rib was made the same. The hut after being erected at Montreuil was eventually sent to Les Attaques, where a further conference was held. The number of roofing sheets was reduced at your suggestion, from five to three. Lt Col Sewell considered that Mr Tarrant (a private contractor) might object to 2 ply covering of the ends and Major Nissen then suggested using vertical boarding with battens over joints...

Nissen received a copy of the above letter, with an accompanying note:-

"As so many months have elapsed since the first Nissen hut took shape, my memory is probably at fault in some particulars. Will you kindly look through the attached and let me know where, if I have gone wrong."

And so Nissen replied to Shelley:- (letter undated.)

"My remembrance of some of the circumstances are slightly different from what you have noted. On verification, I also find that the first two huts are different in detail to your description. I seem to have lost all recollection of your having made any remarks to me before you went to England in April, concerning the development of the hut, although you did make them to me on your return, when you keenly entered into the design I was trying to perfect.

The idea of making a portable hut and the design came to me one day - about April 18th, after you had gone to England on 16th. The next day I had some bows made and a floor started and proceeded with the construction as far as getting the purlins on. At about this time you returned and were very interested over the trouble how to bend the iron and I informed you that a bending machine existed at Ypres. I found out from Col Sims, that we should write to the Chief Engineer, Canadian Corps, for permission to borrow it. In the meantime, while waiting for a reply, you mentioned to General Liddell what we were doing, who said he had such a machine at the Base, which he sent up to us, so we were able to complete the hut. The balance of your memo is quite according to my recollection, with the exception that at the conference at Base Workshops, I suggested that the end panels should be made of unwrought vertical boarding, with the cracks covered by battens. Also, an important point is that Gen Liddell suggested that 3 - 9" sheets should be used instead of the 5 as our first used."

Nissen concludes with a summary of descriptions of the first two huts.

No 1 Hut.

18' long by 18' wide. Three bays, one large window each side or two small ones at each end. A door at each end with a ventilator over each. Lined 5/8" rebated stock boarding. Five sheets iron in circle.

No 2 Hut.

20' long by 18' wide. Three bays, window on each side, or two at each end. Door both ends with ventilator over each. Lined 5/8" rebated boarding which I held was unsatisfactory and advised 1/2" matching. Bows of 4 ply with one narrower to form grove for lining."

Surprisingly, he does not mention No 3 hut, except to remark that; "No 3 hut was moved to Montreuil on June 12th and erected on 13th."

A typed comment by Shelley at the end of Nissen's letter read; "The idea of a semicircular hut was entirely Nissen's own."

Details of No 3 hut are found in what appears to be the final reply to Gen Liddell's search for the history of the hut. Shelley writes to Gen Liddell:-
(Undated, but probably April 1918.)
"Major Nissen undertook to built a third hut with, at his suggestion. 'T' iron bows and at your suggestion a further reduction in width to 16', the height to be 8' and length 27'. The omission of the side windows and adoption of standard doors and windows. It was also agreed to substitute oiled linen for glass in the windows."

And so, after three models a permanent design was agreed. Permanent, that it, apart from relatively minor adaptations according to the function of the hut. The design was never static. The standard model, known as the Nissen Bow Hut was 27 feet long, 16 feet wide and 8 feet high. This was followed by a larger hut of similar design, the Nissen Hospital Hut. 60 feet long, 20 feet wide and about 10 feet high.

No mention, however, as to who first thought of hutting. Events and artifacts are debatable but rarely thoughts, as the history of any subject shows. After Ypres, Nissen organised the transfer of General Headquarters from St Omer to Montreuil, stationed under Lt Col Shelley. Therefore, one could hazard a guess that Nissen could have been the first to suggest hutting. But, surely, the Generals should have been the first to have been aware of such a need ? Indeed, they were there, and had been since the outbreak of war and even before that. Hutting had never been a priority with the War office until after the Anglo-Boer War of 1899-1902, when in January 1907, an earthquake destroyed the entire town of Kingston, Jamaica, in a matter of seconds ! Hospital huts were manufactured and in use by April ! This was followed by the first building of a Flying School at Upavon, on Salisbury Plain in 1912, completed in six months with Armstrong huts, designed by Major B H Armstrong of the War Office, which prompted the writer to remark:-

".....it is not pleasant to think of what might have happened if the construction of this school had followed the 'leisurely trundle' of building operations normal in this country." For this was the training school for the original Royal Flying Corps, the predecessor of the Royal Air Force.

War with Germany was declared on the night of 4th August 1914 and by August 12th Armstrong had issued orders for the construction of hutted camps with the then official Aylwin huts, light framed huts with canvas covering, unsuited for a European war and euphemistically described as 'better than bell tents !' One hut type followed another, the Aylwin gave way to the Armstrong, the Tarrant, the Liddell and finally, late in 1918, the Weblee, which had a roof and wall of steel sheet, a half hexagon hut, if the Nissen can be described as a 'semi circular' design, but it was a 'Nissen' bent to another shape. All hut designs suffered from slavish adherence to a 'house type' hut, with walls and eaves, well suited to peace time conditions, when rapid mass production was not a priority. Hutting was now no longer the concern of the architect but of the engineer. Architectural problems ended with the preparation of plans, but engineering problems were varied and difficult when iron supplanted canvas and wood, requiring a completely different approach to the subject, which Nissen supplied in 1916.

Surprised and disappointed was I, on reading an authoritative article on hutting in the 1914-18 War, in which the Nissen hut, briefly mentioned, was a minor part, compared with the space devoted to other huts. Having

Sgt Robert Donger, Mechanical Draughtsman to Lt. Col. P.N. Nissen R.E.
(Courtesy of Peter Donger.)

known that about 100,000 huts, of his design, had been assembled in France and, having heard of no other hut, I had a deep sense that I was reading about a different war. I then understood the cause of Nissen's sensitivity towards criticisms of his hut by permanent R.E. officers. Lauretta Nissen writes:-

"...there was a good deal of 'feeling' about the hut. The trouble was that Peter was not a regular soldier. It was the business of regular Sappers to provide things like huts, as required, and they tried quite hard to persuade themselves, and other people, that their own plans were quite as good as this rather odd idea coming from a perfectly unknown source." At the same time it must be conceded that Nissen huts were not available in large numbers until September 1916 and, therefore, the gap between August 1914 and September 1916 was filled with peace-time huts, apart from billets in the houses and cottages. Further, the use of galvanised corrugated iron for hut manufacture had been considered at the beginning of the war, but the proposal had been abandoned, because Germany had cornered the world's zinc markets. The advent of the Nissen hut coincided with the unleashing of the two fiercest war machines the world had yet known, heavy artillery and the tank. Casualties and discomfort marked this aspect of prolonged trench warfare, a phase which emphasised the importance of troop morale and it was as important as the standard of arms and equipment. Well organised hospitals and resting accommodation provided a significant support to the British armies and Nissen's contribution of heated huts and hospitals, kitchens, field cookers, drying rooms and shower baths, undoubtedly sustained the discipline and confidence of the British armies engaged in the battles of the Somme from July to September 1916 and the subsequent offensives into the Allied lines planned by General Ludendorff.

Events were now moving fast and soon after Montreuil, there was another move of 45 kilometres south east to Hesdin, a small country town on the river Canche, where Nissen, with two draughtsmen, was preparing plans of hut components for despatch to the United Kingdom manufacturers, but needing mechanical draughtsmen, he applied to Base Records, who found one in Rouen. At a time of national crisis whatever was Corporal Robert Donger R.E. doing in a Post Office ? A case of misdirected talent, perhaps ? Who was this Donger, who became Nissen's right hand man throughout the latter half of the Great War ? Born in 1892, in Ipswich, his family moved to Manchester, where he attended a primary school, followed by evening classes in such subjects as Arithmetic, Machine Construction and Drawing, Workshop

Practice and Practical Mathematics, obtaining a first class certificate in each of them. Then to an apprenticeship with Vickers Armstrong Company, at Trafford Park, Manchester. Truly an excellent training for the work upon which he was to embark with Nissen, but more remarkable that in the maelstrom of modern warfare two such professionally complementary characters should find themselves working together as a technical unit !

Donger's hobbies were photography and water colours, especially when on holiday in North Wales, Cheshire and the Isle of Man. He had volunteered for service at the outbreak of war, but almost two years were to pass before joining Nissen, now a Major. Draughtmanship was not his only skill; he wrote an eleven foolscap page account of his association with Nissen at Hesdin, in a lively, readable and relaxed conversational style with which I cannot even hope to compete as it was an 'on the spot reporting'. So, the bulk of the hut story during World War I is seen through the eyes of Robert Donger:-

"Hesdin is a barrack town and contains a cavalry barracks with an infantry barracks and hospital combined. The entire town was in the British zone and 29th Field Company R.E. occupied the hospital block in the infantry barracks which was used as offices and men's billets, the yard being given over to workshops which contained a gas engine for generating power to drive the machinery such as circular saws, band saws, a forge and tinsmith's shop.

My introduction to Major Nissen was of the regimental order and, needless to say, was conducted by the Sergeant Major. "Quick March ! Right turn ! Halt ! Yes !" Some of the old soldiers found it impossible to live except 'by numbers !' A mode of life I heartily detested and, I believe, the O.C. did, too, being more concerned with getting on with the job, than with the etiquette of the army."

"I was soon put at ease and pottered about the workshops for a day or two and was then called to the drawing office where two draughtsmen were already engaged. The Major invited me to go through all the hut details with him. He had in mind a scheme for issuing erection instructions which would be foolproof and enable anyone with only a merest spark of intelligence to successfully erect a Nissen hut. This was accomplished by making diagrammatic drawings, showing each stage of the erection and marked up, giving all operations in sequence. These drawings were printed in thousands and a copy was packed with the fitting for each hut."

"The next problem to tackle was compactness in packing a hut for road travel. Most lorries in use at the time had a dead weight capacity of three tons and, although the hut was under this weight, its bulk, if not packed with a little pre-thought, was too great for the lorry and it was discovered that three lorries were required to transport two huts. To solve the difficulty a few experimental attempts were made with our own company lorry and the most economical system was soon found. The materials were left in the lorry and a sketch made and then another fool-proof diagram was produced and the copies distributed in their thousands, throughout the armies. The diagram illustrated every part of the hut and every part had an index letter and a description giving the order in which the parts should be put into a three ton lorry, leaving room for three men also; thus a great saving in transport was brought about, which was of inestimable value in those days.

"The Nissen hut was now very much an established fact. Instructions for every contingency having been issued in regard to packing, for economic transport, erection, dismantling and the idea of having huts made in England being mooted by the War Office, who now had all the working drawings. The idea was very soon exploited and firms all over the country were soon busily engaged. Joinery firms such as Boulton and Paul of Norwich and the Thames Joinery Company making panels. Wm Baird & Co, of Coatbridge making steel ribs and John Summers & Co and Brady & Co, producing corrugated sheets, whilst the Black Country nut and bolt manufacturers had a busy time."

"During November 1916, several minor stunts were thought out which proved very successful. A Drying Hut was produced, which consisted of a tower about eight feet square and about twenty feet high. This was constructed of carton bitumen (an equivalent to many of the roofing felts in use in England.) nailed to a framework of 2" x 2" deal. The carton bitumen served a double purpose, it saved timber, which was becoming scarce and, therefore, valuable and it was a non-conductor of heat and prevented the heat from escaping from the drying tower. The heat was obtained simply from a four inch diameter stove pipe passing through the centre of the tower and out of the top. In other words a long chimney fed by a fire lighted in a pit outside the tower. Clothes were hung on everything convenient - nails, screws or pegs, which could be fixed to the rails which formed the framework."

"Shower baths were now produced, with hot and cold water, providing both water and fire were available. The experiment was carried out with two small beer barrels, a few feet of steel tubing and the necessary roses with levers and chains for the showers. The fire pit was dug in the ground, generally circular and lined with bricks, if available ! A conical sheet iron

Above. Unloading a truck with Nissen hut components. H40791
Below. Wooden joists have been screwed to the bearers and are ready to receive the wooden floor panels. IWM 2099

Above. Fixing the light interior corrugated iron. Note the fabric sheet between the corrugated sheets for greater heat insulation. IWM 2101
Below. Fixing the exterior sheets of corrugated iron. IWM 2099

Above. Major P N Nissen on a tour of inspection. Q 1743
Below. Members of the Women's Army Auxiliary Corps (WAAC) in their Nissen hut.H 40806

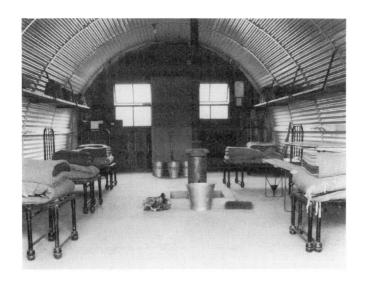

Above. Interior of a Nissen hut. Note the 'telescoped' beds, the Canadian stove and the goods rack. This is probably a hospital hut. H 21381

Below. Lt Col P.N. Nissen escorts Her Majesty Queen Mary during her inspection of a Nissen hut in France. Q 2529

All eight photos, courtesy of the Imperial War Museum.

cover surmounted the pit, with a door for fuelling. The cone terminated in a collar to which the stove pipe was attached. The fire thrived on rubbish due to a fierce draught induced by a pipe led down from above the ground to the bottom of the pit. The pipe was provided with a regulating shutter at the top and the draught could therefore be regulated to the combustible quality of the fuel."

"Sheet iron stoves were largely used in offices and billets on the same 'down draught' principle and the troops guaranteed these stoves to 'burn shaving water !' If my memory is correct, Col Nissen told me that he brought the idea from the Canadian backwoods."

"Reverting to the Shower Baths, there was nothing unique in the system and no claim was ever advanced, but they were an object lesson in improvisation and showed how, by application of thought, a conglomeration of odds and ends, and even materials which were apparently useless, could be adapted to serve such useful purposes. The baths were received with acclamation and corrugated iron tanks of about one hundred gallons capacity were ordered in thousands and issued to all army stores. Lithographic copies of our drawings were produced in large numbers and distributed throughout the armies. Sapper Kelsey. R.E. and Private Newton. Artists Rifles collaborated in making the drawings."

"Meanwhile, the Major had produced an oven, or field cooker. This was known as a 'three tier' oven, the name being self-explanatory. It was made of sheet iron and the three ovens were graded in size, the largest one at the bottom and the smallest at the top. The ovens did not rest directly upon each other, but were spaced with a cavity between the top of the one and the bottom of the next. Similarly, a cavity, or passage about 4" wide was formed at the sides and the heat, consisting generally of smoke and hot gases produced by the fuel, passed under the lower oven, then up by its side, over the top into the cavity or passage under the second oven, up by the side of the second oven, then under the bottom of the top oven and continuing up by the side and over the top and passing away in the chimney. The fire, as for the baths and the drying towers was contained in a pit dug in the ground. Thousands of these ovens were used in the field and even in rest camps and were capable of roasting a joint, baking a milk pudding and producing first class pastry simultaneously. They proved very popular with army cooks !"

As if that were not enough, Nissen proceeded to invent what he named a 'Mud-punt'. A carrier for transporting shells from the dump to the guns. An old Ford car engine was mounted on a wooden platform at the centre of a

96

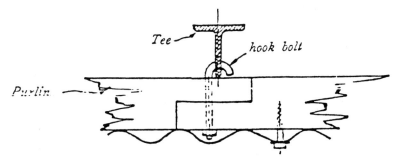

The Hook-Bolt: Hook-bolts are mentioned when describing how a Nissen hut is erected. The diagram helps to explain how a purlin is attached to the tee of a bow by a hook-bolt by first inserting the hook through a hole in the tee. The wavy line represents the outer covering of corrugated iron. (The 'Nissen' Standard Building, Royal Engineers Journal, Nov. 1920, 221-224) Courtesy of the Royal Engineers Institution.

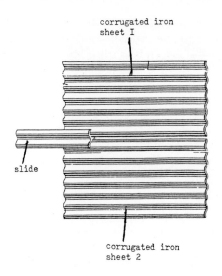

corrugated iron sheet I

slide

corrugated iron sheet 2

The slide consisted of a double piece of corrugated iron, 7 feet long and 6 inches wide, fixed in the centre by a rivet. The sketch shows how the slide is applied.

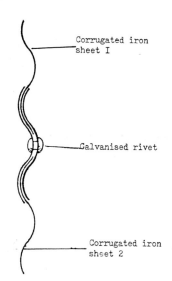

Corrugated iron sheet I

Galvanised rivet

Corrugated iron sheet 2

A cross-sectional view of the slide. It was invented in order to join the iron sheets which were used to make an inner lining for the hut.

Nissen's Invention of the "SLIDE" or "JOINTING PIECE" for joining corrugated iron sheets. (from various Patent applications, e.g. No. 194205 of Nov 25th 1919, Patent Office, Toronto. Canada.)

punt-shaped raft in the floor of which were two holes. A chain passed through one hole, then over a 30 inch diameter grooved wheel to which steel pads were added so that the wheel could grip the chain links, then out through the second hole. In principle it was a caterpillar tractor, with a limited travel equal to the length of the chain. The operator started the engine and the shells were transported to the guns, automatically stopping as the end of the chain was reached when the engine was switched off by the operator. After unloading, the engine was put in reverse and then off to the dump for a further supply of shells. The story of the 'Mud-punt' becomes vague when Corporal Donger entered hospital at Etaples with nephritis, from which he fortunately recovered, but it is known that Mud-punts were manufactured in the United Kingdom, with 100 horse powered engines.

Alas ! The Nissen saga now ran into difficulties. In spite of carefully printed instructions on erecting the hut, some were erected without following them. In some cases the hook bolts were driven through the corrugated iron sheets, leaving them no longer waterproof. No reason is stated, but it might be assumed that the lack of hanging devices in lieu of wardrobes was the excuse! The wooden ends of some huts were not tarred but instead, they were banked around with earth which was never removed in the warmer Spring and summer. But the chief sin occurred in areas where firewood was lacking, so that in winter, the matchboarding lining was ripped out and burnt as required, thus reducing the efficiency of the hut as a billet. Nissen sought an inflammable lining and what better than corrugated iron ? An easy solution ? But how to fix the sheets on the inside of the hut ? The external sheets had been easily fixed to the purlins, the rows of wood which formed part of the hut framework, but there was nothing to which the inside sheets could be fixed, unless it was to the underside of the purlins. "Far too complicated !" said Nissen. His solution was to use straight lengths of corrugated iron and fix them to the frame in a horizontal position. But then the sheets would not span the distance between the purlins ! As Donger put it;- "The Major pottered about in the tinsmith's shop with a few pieces of corrugated iron." He emerged with a 'slide', a double piece of corrugated iron about 7 feet by 6 inches wide, fixed in the centre by a rivet. This was made to slide between the two pieces of corrugated iron, as shown in the sketch, which explains it better. An exhibition hut was constructed and the hierarchy of General Headquarters invited to view it, including sceptics who likened it to a refrigerator. However, thermometers were put in each of the two huts, one with a corrugated lining and the other with a matchboard lining. They only registered half a degree Fahrenheit difference in temperature ! Didn't they learn at school that air is a poor conductor of heat ? Donger resumes his story:-

"Drawings of the slide were now made and rushed to England where slides were turned out as quickly as possible, mostly (I think) by John Summers & Co, of Shotten, Chester and in a very short time all consignments of Nissen huts from England were provided with corrugated iron linings and slides."

"Her Majesty, the Queen was very interested in this new venture and when she visited the hospital, now established in our barracks, made a special inspection of this self-same hut. Incidentally, it transpired that this hut was the most cosy in our camp during the winter and, decidedly, the coolest in summer !" The discovery of the slide was of extreme importance, for in this article alone lies the patent which was obtained soon after the war had ended. Lauretta Nissen adds a little more to the very brief account of the Queen's visit to Hesdin.

"Peter used to speak of the Queen's visit. It was his duty to rig up a dressing table for her in the Chateau, where she stayed the night. He contrived a tasty affair with a packing case and some muslin - at least he was very proud of it. He was much impressed by the Queen's kindliness and very intelligent interest she showed in all she saw. He said she asked a number of very sensible questions."

So much for the hut from an 'insiders' view, from one who saw and took part in its evolution. What of its impact on one seeing it for the first time? Filson Young, a Daily Mail journalist, supplied a delightful account for the newspaper's issue of February 6th 1917, although his quantities seem incorrect:-

"At about the same time as the tanks made their memorable debut on the battlefield, another creature, almost equally primaeval of aspect, began to appear in conquered areas. No one ever saw it on the move, or met it on the roads. It just appeared ! Overnight you would see a blank space of ground. In the morning it would be occupied by an immense creature of the tortoise species, settled down solidly and permanently on the earth, and emitting green smoke from a right angled system at one end, where its mouth might be, as though it were smoking a morning pipe. And when such a pioneer found that the situation was good and the land habitable, it would pass the word, for by twos and threes, by tens and hundreds, its fellow monsters would appear,

100

so that in a week or two you would find a valley covered with them that had been nothing but pulverised earth before.

"The name of this creature is the Nissen hut. It is the solution of one of the many problems that every war presents. The problem here was to devise a cheap, portable dwelling place, wherein men can live, warm and dry. Simple enough to be erected by anybody on any ground........ He (Nissen) did his preliminary thinking so well that the third hut he built is of the pattern being used now., of which there are at least 20,000 in France today..... The Nissen hut has no walls, it consists of a roof, ends and a floor. The roof is simply an arch of corrugated iron so that there are no eaves or gables to fit. Anyone can put it up, but four men can do it easily in four hours. The only tool required - a spanner - is supplied with it ! The whole can be packed on an army wagon and its weight is two tons, but no single part or package is heavier than that which can be unloaded by two men. All parts are interchangeable - the roof is in 28 pieces - all the same. You arrange them in three 9 foot sheets with one corrugation overlap. You go on fitting them together, anyhow, in any order and when they are all used up, you find the roof complete. The lining of half inch matchboard is fastened to ribs of 'T' iron that follow the semi circular shape of the roof. There are five ribs made of three segments each. These segments are nested in bundles of five, you use them in any order you like - they are all the same !"

"There are no nails to drive. A single pattern of hookbolt is used for every fastening. The lining is tongued and grooved, and however green the wood is or however much it may shrink owing to the heat in the hut there are no draughts. You simply keep knocking it down tight to the sides of the hut (where the men's heads are when they are asleep) and the shrinkage is represented by an open space along the middle of the roof, which gives ventilation into the air space between the roof and the ceiling, which is so valuable a feature of the hut. It keeps the heat in in winter and out in summer."

"These are the new homes for which many a soldier on the Somme front is thanking his stars in this bitter weather. By day the beds are rolled up against the sides and the whole middle space is available for work, games, messing, reading and writing. The hut is warmed by the ordinary Canadian stove - an iron drum with two holes in it and a smoke pipe - which is the only portable furnace that you can make red hot on green wood fuel. The Nissen hut will not keep out shells, but its round back lends itself to the most artistic camouflage. In short, among the creatures to which the War has given birth, it

Hesdin, Pas de Calais, perhaps? Huts accommodating Nissen's workmen. The duckboards over muddy ground confirm the impression that Nissen was a perfectionist. (Photo Robert Donger, kindly lent by his son, Peter Donger.)

102

has already earned a high character as a useful, tractable, kindly domestic beast. Some officers in high commands think so highly of it as to make collections of it, so that there is scarcely a chateau which houses an army or corps headquarters but has two or three perfectly tame ones crouching within sight of the front door and acting with equal docility as telephone exchanges, map rooms, stables or offices."

"Of course, being the British Army, there were hosts of jokes about them, such as; 'One of them huts you sit down in, but couldn't lean back !' Or, the father on meeting his son on leave; "Well, my boy, the cares of the War seem to be weighing heavily on your shoulders." "It's not that, Dad. I've been living in a Nissen hut for two or three months - I'll soon straighten out !"

Nissen was, of course, aware of the many remarks about his hut - complimentary or otherwise - and when addressing the Engineering Society at Queen's University in Canada in 1920, he thought himself the 'most maligned man in the British Army.' And, having heard such dreadful things about the Nissen Hut, he apologised for ever having invented it.

Did the Germans have their own 'Nissen' hut ? A question which, I think, follows naturally in this chapter. Official sources are few. First, the *Handbuch für Heer und Flotte* (Army and Navy handbook) of 1909 is most informative, three closely printed pages, about temporary huts from 1807 onwards, beginning with the aftermath of the battle of Eylau in Prussia, when Napoleon's army routed the Russians who had aided Prussia in its forlorn attempt to stem the French advance across Europe. Later, in 1870-71, huts were used in the battles for Metz and Sedan in the Franco-Prussian War. Later still, Germany's search for colonies encouraged their use in Manchuria and German South West Africa (Namibia). Construction materials are mentioned, stone, tiles, concrete blocks, timber, asbestos, 'felt-board', canvas, wood and corrugated iron, but it is not quite understood as to which of these materials were used for each type of hut. Yet there is no doubt that these huts were never used for the relaxation and recovery of soldiers resting between battles as was the case with the British and French armies, but for the hospitalisation of the sick and wounded, with special emphasis on the 'quarantining' of service men returning from overseas campaigns who may have contracted cholera, smallpox or leprosy. So German hutting has a long history of its own, but because we are more concerned with the first World War, a partial answer to my question is supplied by *Der gros Krieg 1914-18* (The Great War 1914-

103

18) by M. Schwarte (no date of publication.) The field hospitals are now larger than in previous wars and the furious attention to pests and infectious diseases is probably greater. We read of a converted school where they 'managed to delouse close to 1,800 men per day !' - Such hygienic details bear little resemblance to the functions of the Nissen huts and, therefore, I was relieved to receive some personal comments from my German military informant at the School of Infantry at Hammelburg, East of Frankfurt. He tells of the Bernhard-Grove Hut and the Doker Hut and thinks he finds the former comparable with the Nissen Hut, because it had a wood foundation with walls and roof of corrugated iron, but there the correspondence ends . The Doker and the Wutsdorff, named after their designers, were entirely wooden huts. They came with vertical walls and gabled roofs, and were supplied in parts ready for assembling. From the little information at hand it appears that the German designers could not succeed in cracking the normal house-plan mould as did Nissen. Ah well ! Some information, but sadly lacking in detail. Oh for a German Corporal Donger !

Accidents with Mills bombs were common during both World Wars, especially as they were thrown by hand. There was a time when two teaching acquaintances suffered injuries as a result of accidental blasts at bomb practice, one with terrible injuries to his reproductive parts and the other mentally changed from a quiet introspective type to a brash extrovert. Both victims of bombs dropped at practice after the safety pin had been removed. They were lucky as some in their units were killed by the blasts. Removing the safety pin released a plunger which caused the bomb to become live and burst on contact with the ground. Nissen redesigned the bomb so that the plunger was supported by a coil of thread which unwound when the bomb was thrown, because the free end of the thread was attached to a key-ring held by the thrower. On throwing the bomb the thread unwound and, at a safe distance, now free of the thread, the pressure on the plunger was released which now rendered the bomb live. Unfortunately, the British War Office could not finance the cost of a new plant for bomb production, yet Nissen was able to make experimental bomb casts in a foundry at the Royal Engineers workshop in Montreuil and tested his bombs, both safely and successfully.

With the ever increasing pace of warfare the number of wounded requiring attention also increased and so the Hesdin headquarters became such a large hospital that Donger's artistic skills were used in painting a forest

104

of sign-boards indicating the various wards and facilities such as are found in hospitals today. Nissen and his Engineers were then transferred to Montreuil, 15 miles north west of Hesdin, where he produced what proved to be his last invention of the war, again best described by Robert Donger:-

"About 8 o'clock one morning in March (1918), the Colonel's batman called me to the Colonel's billet. There I found him in pyjamas, stropping a razor. He had conceived the idea with his waking thoughts, apparently, and I was given the outline of a new type of building, later to be known as the 'Nissen Patent Steel Tent' Details were committed to paper during the day and the drawings handed over to the 29th Company workshop, where a tent was made during the next few days, in secrecy. A day or so later, the sappers took the materials along to the Ecole Militaire in the small hours of the morning. It should be understood that the Ecole Militaire was a vast training college for officers in peace time and had been taken over by the British as the 'Holy of Holies' and was the chief administrative centre of the British Armies in France. It contained hundreds of offices and departments and also housed many of the troops who were employed within its confines. It also contained a quadrangle used for drill and parades."

"On this particular morning, when the troops began to bestir themselves and leave their billets to make for the ablution sheds which were dotted about around the sides of the quadrangle, they stopped in amazement before an unexpected apparition. Yes ! The sappers had done their work well and, commencing their job at dawn, had put the whole tent together and laid a wooden floor, by the time full daylight had arrived. For men who were accustomed to surprises, the occupants of the Ecole Militaire showed remarkable interest and we had a fine tableau of the 'Brains of the Army', with towels round their necks and bits of soap in their hands, inspecting the tent in relays. The Engineer-in-Charge and the Deputy General of Medical Services were in the secret and, with many other staff officers, made an inspection during the day.. Not one word of criticism was uttered and hearty congratulations were freely offered to Col Nissen. A requisition was made out the same day for 2,000 tents. Working drawings were now prepared for the War office so that manufacture could take place on an elaborate scale in England."

"The tent needs no description here, for it has become a familiar sight throughout our countryside and, almost without exception, those tents we see dotted about the fields, are replicas of the original erected on that March morning. Too late, however, for war-time use. German advances meant considerable loss of hutting with other equipment and the War Office thought that the Nissen Tent intended for 20 men was a convenient replacement, but the War came to an end before it could be used in France."

What happened to the Nissen Steel tents ? Where are they now ? Robert Donger writes of them in 1930 as 'a familiar sight throughout the countryside ....dotted about the fields." I have yet to see one but from a diagram on Nissen's application form for the Patent, 'it consists of an upright cylinder of corrugated iron, diameter about 22 feet, surmounted by a conical roof of flat iron, the whole about 15 feet high, mounted on a concrete base with a door and two windows. Those with long memories may have seen them, but the 'tents' are no longer standing. A friend spent a holiday with his wife in two 'tents' joined together on Ham Island on the Thames near Windsor in 1952 and a 'tent' was delivered to Nissen at his last home on Westerham Hill in 1921 - I have seen the broken remains. The use of ungalvanised iron may have caused them to rust away. It was widely known that there was a world-wide shortage of zinc, exacerbated by the hoarding of this metal by Germany before the 1914-18 war. Yet even at this late hour I would be happy to see a 'Nissen Steel Tent'.

The last stages of the War must have proved an anti-climax for Nissen. Enemy air raids on Montreuil had caused a move to Wailly-Beauchamp, five miles away, where his skills were no longer required for hutting and so in June 1918 he was given the command of a Royal Engineers Company, attached to a District Independent Force of the Royal Air Force, further south near Nancy, whilst Corporal Donger stayed on at Wailly. Their Armistice celebrations on November 11th 1918 could hardly have been more disparate. Donger notes:-

"At General headquarters, the general impression now prevailed that the war could not last much longer and as our work was constructive and not destructive, work was not taken very seriously. Considerable time was spent in finding a suitable flagpole and erecting it in front of the office and on November 11th, the troops gathered round during the hoisting of the Union Jack amid the firing of a few revolvers, pointing harmlessly to the sky. We took the precaution of placing an armed guard round the workshops as the troops, in a convivial mood, may have considered that a great bonfire would be an effective termination to a great day and 'What was the use of wartime workshops now anyway ?" Nissen's recollections of that day are conveyed in Lauretta's notes:-

106

"It so happened that they were stationed next to an Italian Regiment, and Peter had been asked to have dinner in the Italian Mess, in honour of the King's of Italy's birthday on November 11th. On that marvellous day, Peter had a violent cold in his head. He remembered sitting beside the Italian Colonel, feeling absolutely light-headed and getting more and more drunk as did also the little Italian. At every moment he would turn to Peter and cry 'Viva l'Lughhilterra !' and drain his glass. Peter responded with "Viva Italia !" and drained his. - The little Colonel flung his arms round Peter's neck and embraced him warmly - and then Da Capo !"

Nissen returned home for good on the last day of 1918 and was demobilised on 24th February 1919, according to Lauretta Nissen . But, the last official mention in the Army List appeared in June 1920. Meanwhile, the Foreign Orders List of the War Office for November 1919, reveals that he was awarded the Order of St Sava, 3rd Class, by the Serbian Government. Due, no doubt, to the civil war in Yugo-Slavia, I have been unable to discover the citation which normally accompanies such an award. For his hutting inventions he had received the Distinguished Service Order (DSO) and also Mentioned in Despatches, a form of letter commending the work of the person mentioned, made by a superior officer.

Did the end of the war signal the demise of the Nissen Hut ? It had performed the tasks assigned to it as a wartime exercise, with little or no reference to peacetime activities. What of the huts left in France and Belgium, about 100,000 of them belonging to the War Office ? And those in England, still in the process of manufacture ? What temptations abounded when such property had a sale value - and by a War office which never paid the inventor a penny, nor had any intention of doing so ! How did the hut quietly survive, ready at hand for further wartime service in the Second World War 1939-45 and the Falklands War of 1982. In the following chapter an attempt will be made to unravel the various strands of the tapestry of failure and success, of adaptation and innovation, of architectural disdain and of bureaucratic cover up. Meanwhile, Nissen in 1921 became a United Kingdom citizen by naturalisation.

Having subjected the reader to the technicalities of the Nissen Hut, perhaps one is justified in completing this chapter on a more leisurely note, by including an extract from an account written by a Japanese about 800 years ago, without emphasising the similarities between Chomei's grass hut and Nissen's steel hut, their simplicity and their mobility. Well ! Here it is:-

"Now that I have reached the age of sixty and my life seems to evaporate like the dew, I have fashioned a lodging for the last leaves of my years. It is a hut where, perhaps, a traveller might spend a single night; it is like the cocoon spun by an aged silkworm. This hut is not even a hundredth the size of a cottage where I spent my middle years."

"Before I was aware, I had become heavy with years and with each remove my dwelling grew smaller. The present hut is of no ordinary appearance, it is a bare ten feet square and less than seven feet high. I did not choose this particular spot, rather than another, and I built my house without consulting any diviners. I laid a foundation and a roughly thatched roof. I fastened hinges to the joints of the beams, the easier to move elsewhere should anything displease me. What difficulty would there be in changing my dwelling ? A bare two carts would suffice to carry off the whole house and except for the carter's fee, there would be no expenses at all."

(from 'An Account of My Hut' by Kamo no Chomei, 1153-1216 - a Buddhist priest, taken from *Anthology of Japanese Literature* by Donald Keense, Penguin Books 1968) By permission of Grove/Atlantic Inc. New York.

And finally, a few statistics from the Imperial War Museum at Duxford, Cambs.

Supplied to France and Belgium:

Bow Huts   100,000 to accommodate 2,400,000 men
Hospital Huts   10,000 to accommodate 240,000 beds
The first Nissen Bow Hut to be inspected - 15th May 1916
First orders to be placed for manufacture in England, August 1916
Normal time of erection by 6 men - 4 hours
Record time - 1 hour 27 minutes.

6. THE HUT LIVES ON

"...People seek an individual problem for their
social problem, and so ultimately create
a second problem." Lewis Mumford.
The Social Foundations of Post-War Building. 1943

The previous chapter closed on a hint of official scandal. All can now be revealed. It was an attempt by the minions of government to deprive Nissen of a suitable reward for his inventions used in the War, although he was aware that whilst serving in the British Army, he had no claim on Government funds. But as Lauretta explains in her notes:-

"It is usual for the War Office to give the inventor a sum of money in consideration of his invention. Eventually, Peter was offered £500. In view of the great number of huts manufactured, Peter thought this sum to be inadequate. He was hurt by the offer and refused to accept the money."

But although inventions may yield an uncertain reward, there is no uncertainty about the means by which they can be protected. And he knew this. Nissen's reputation and experience stamped him as an inventor and like any sensible innovator, he protected his inventions by using the services of a professional patent agent to draw up the application. His regular agent was the family firm of Phillip's of 70 Chancery Lane, London. WC, followed by an expert scrutiny at the hands of a solicitor, Walter John Chamberlain of Chamberlain and Company, also a family firm of 1 Stone Buildings, Lincolns Inn, London. WC. How and where Nissen met Chamberlain is not recorded, but undoubtedly a meeting of entrepreneurial minds of about the same age; mature and young, yet decisive. It is possible that they first met in 1910 when Chamberlain forwarded Nissen's Stamp Mill application to the Patent Office in London. Chamberlain's varied concerns were with the Hairdressers' Associations, the allotments of the Horticultural Societies, the Blind, the Boy Scouts. He was Clerk of the Fine Arts Trades of Great Britain and, above all, he was an Alderman of the Croydon Borough Council and he had served two terms as Mayor. A sample of his vigorous language is illustrated by his reference, on one occasion, to the overlordship of Whitehall.

"I am sure you are all labouring under a mistaken view that majorities should rule. It seems that minorities can rule when a minority of one sitting in Whitehall can dictate to fifty-six aldermen and councillors, elected by 200,000 people in Croydon. Nothing can persuade me that that can be right !"

For his approaching campaign against the Government for illegal hut sales, Nissen could not have found a better fighter than Chamberlain.

The Nissen Bow Hut, to give its official title and the larger Nissen Hospital Hut, were invented in April 1916, followed by applications to patent in June 1916, such applications being made with Government permission. Government permission was also sought and granted to patent the huts in certain overseas countries e.g. Australia, Canada, New Zealand, Union of South Africa, Russia, the Argentine Republic, the USA, Belgium and France. The interest in this list was in the possible accumulation of abandoned huts in France and Belgium which could be sold in these countries when war had ceased. But, immediately, it should have been possible to sell huts to the USA. Or was it possible ? The original agreement, or Principle Indenture, signed by Nissen, Chamberlain and the Secretary of State for the War Office, on April 25th 1917, made no mention of USA supplies, in spite of the rights accorded to Nissen through his patents. So why not go forward and offer huts to the USA Government ? The US Military Attaché in London and the American Purchasing Agency were approached and supplies ordered but soon cancelled because it was found that the British Government had already supplied the US Government with 1,800 huts and had accepted a further order for 1,000 and therefore, they said, there was no necessity for the US Government to deal with Nissen. Nissen protested about his financial loss to the Secretary of State to the Treasury on two occasions, in October and November 1918. Protests which received no reply.

Regretfully, these letters cannot be traced by the present Treasury Office. There may appear to be an ethical objection to Nissen receiving royalties, whilst the war was in progress but, "It is desired to make it quite plain." wrote Chamberlain, "that Col Nissen makes no complaint whatever either of infringement of his American patent by the British Government or of their

110

action in selling to the US Government, he having been more than willing for the US Government to have the benefits of his huts without any strict rights, so long as the war was going on; the only question is, of course, payment to him in respect of what has been done."

Sales of huts to the USA were not the only cause for complaint. The war, having finished, the British Government was found selling huts to the governments of France and Belgium, huts left permanently in those countries, of which 5,500 had already been sold to the Belgian Government. This was too much for Chamberlain.

Chamberlain, as a man of the world, probably realised that the action of one man against the Government was bound to fail, however right its cause, unless he could enlist the interest, sympathy and the 'clout' of an 'Establishment Man' and this he found in Sir Alexander Lawrence, (1861-1943) Chief of Staff to the Commander in Chief, the British Army, General Sir Douglas Haig. To quote from the memorandum from Chamberlain to Lawrence:-
"The suggestions advanced therefore are:-

1. That Col Nissen be paid £1 per hut manufactured so far as used by or for the British Government.
2. That he be paid a royalty of £3.10.0. per hut on all huts sold to the United States.
3. That he be paid a like royalty on all new huts sold to any other of the Allied Governments during the process of the war."

One may have mixed feelings, a sense of ambivalence about these suggestions, yet charitably conclude that they emanated from Chamberlain, rather than Nissen, who, appeared to be demanding royalties from Governments left in sore financial straits after a prolonged war. Nissen, speaking to a reporter from the *Pittsburgh Sun* (June 5th 1917) "And, after the war, there would be homes for the homeless of France. The huts can be moved anywhere." The two men appeared to agree that 'If the British Government is as kind hearted as the average Tommy, it will give the 'bloomin arf cartwheels' (as the huts were called) to the Frenchies."

111

With regard to new huts stored in England, Nissen was prepared to purchase these as required at a price named by the War Office, to which he would add a royalty of £5 per hut, about which there could be no ambivalence as such huts were now a commercial venture unrelated to the promotion of war. The response to the memorandum was a Supplementary Indenture of May 22nd 1919 by His Majesty's Principal Secretary of State for the War Department, in which it displayed, perhaps surprisingly, an unyielding stubbornness over the definition of 'right of user' - 'shall be read and construed as if in addition to granting the right of user it had granted the right to sell any part-worn or other stocks of Nissen huts except to the Government of the United States of America.'

But for Nissen, the good news ! In reply to his agreement to recognise the new definition of 'right of user', there was to be a payment to Nissen of £10,000 free of Income Tax - much better than the original award of £500 ! For the huts already sold to the United States Government, the Secretary of State would 'use his best endeavours' to obtain from the purchaser, for the inventor, the sum of £3.10.0. for each Bow Hut and £10.0.0. for each Hospital Hut. It appears that the British Government was aware that it was now an ongoing collecting agent for Nissen's USA royalties and so introduced another Supplementary Indenture of November 24th 1920 granting him a sum of £3,500 to waive any claim for royalties from the British Government, but Lauretta Nissen believed that he received £13,400, not as royalties but as a capital sum. I shall leave this incident with Lauretta's remark:-
"Chamberlain stuck to his guns and showed fight !"

If there was ever a hint that the Nissen hut might outlast the War, it was to be found in a letter to the *Spectator*, of unknown date, sent from France by a member of the British Expeditionary Force:-
"In the reconstruction after the war, we are looking forward to a gigantic task of building and rebuilding houses for the people, not only in the devastated parts of France and Belgium, but also in our own land. As regards England and Scotland, the work must be done quickly and, therefore, probably badly and inartistically, at the expense of the State, and at a huge expense, owing to the scarcity of labour and building materials. But it is not always realised that a change has come over the minds of those who have served in the army and who are destined owners of the new houses. There are millions of officers and men who have lived for years in Nissen huts, tents,

112

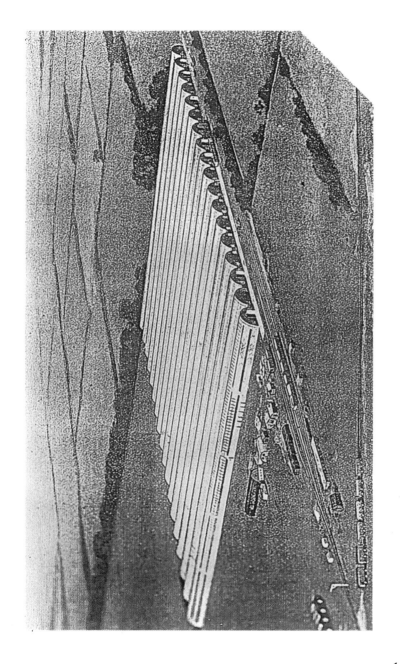

Aerial view of the National Wool Sheds near Hull which covered nearly 10 acres. 1921-30. (*"Nissen" Patent Steel Buildings*, a booklet promoting products of Nissen Buildings Ltd.) (courtesy of Schreiber Furniture Ltd - From the collection of P.C.M. Nissen)

Nissen Buildings Ltd, at Hoddesdon, Hertfordshire today, the industrial ruin of a company which ceased functioning in 1977. (courtesy of Mr Peter Donger, Hertford.)

shacks and shelters and those who have at any time possessed a share in a well-warmed Nissen hut during a cold French winter, have found themselves sufficiently comfortable to declare that they are no longer willing to spend from one tenth to one fifth, or even one fourth, of their income in rent of a cottage or small dwelling. At the close of the war there will be available a very large number of such huts which will probably be disposed of to contractors at a few shillings apiece. Could not they be utilised, especially in country districts and would they not be accepted by men who have learned that such a hut is cheap and good and who have got rid of old fashioned prejudices in favour of stone or lime or brick houses, which cost a great deal and, when badly built, are poor enough shelters ? As a temporary measure to tide over the first five or ten years of scarcity and strain, this might be considered. Certainly, it is curious how often one hears among the men in France; "I never want to bother about a house again, when I can have something like this and save a great deal of my money." I am, Sir, etc,..

The editor's note;- "As a temporary shelter - yes', may have echoed the suburban taste of *Spectator* readers, further emphasised by; 'But, after all, house pride is part of the art of life that cannot be cultivated in a Nissen hut.' The British 'Tommy' living under difficult conditions could be excused in forgetting the costs of sub-division of huts, installing the necessary plumbing and heating and, above all, the reactions of Mrs 'Tommy'

Had there been a demand for such housing after the war, Nissen was well qualified and experienced to satisfy it. In 1914 he had founded Nissen's Ltd, in London. A contracting building company which was forced to cease activities when war was declared and then reopened after the war in Corporation Street, Birmingham. But first he planned to revisit relations and friends in the United States and Canada. Whilst away from England his manager, Wright Cox, obtained a magnificent contract to build the National Wool Sheds at Hull for storing, primarily, the 1921 Australian wool crop, or 'clip' as it is called. The extent of this complex of Nissen type buildings can be appreciated from the aerial photograph, occupying almost ten acres under one roof and chosen because it was near to the wool factories of Yorkshire. It was additional to a three acre wool warehouse at the King George Dock on the River Humber. This massive accumulation and storage of Australian wool dates from 1916 under the Imperial Wool Purchase Scheme by which raw wool was stored in England to prevent supplies reaching Germany, but at the

A 1930s view of Rye House station, with part of the Nissen Buildings Ltd, seen in the background. (courtesy of National Monuments Record.)

Nissen-Petren houses at West Camel, Somerset. Four Non-Parlour houses are seen in the foreground; whilst those beyond are Parlour houses. (courtesy of Margaret Payne, Westerham.)

117

end of the war there was an embarrassingly excessive stock-pile of wool which demanded not only an enormous increase in storage capacity but to be provided quickly. The Nissen method of building was the answer. - 18 immense sheds, each 552 feet long and 40 feet wide with a total storage capacity of 234,000 bales - too difficult to visualise ! The Australian portion of this stockpile was sold off by a company formed for the purpose, the British-Australian Wool Realization Association Limited (BAWRA) which began operations on January 1st 1921 and finished in May 1924. Apart from the Australian contribution there were bales from New Zealand, South Africa, the Falklands, United States and, surprisingly, from a large number of European countries. Thereafter, the sheds were disused and then removed in about 1930. The site is now part of a housing estate.

The National Wool Sheds contract proved a valuable source of capital, and on Nissen's return to England he was able, in 1922, to mortgage several adjoining fields at Rye House, Hoddesdon, Hertfordshire, which lay between the River Lea and the railway to London. The original Rye House had its hour of doubtful glory in 1693 when Charles II was reigning and his Tory 'Popish' Parliament was harassing Protestant Dissenters. Former Roundhead soldiers from Cromwell's army planned to waylay and murder the King and his brother (afterwards James II) on their return to Rye House from the Newmarket Races. The plot was discovered and the culprits executed. Today, the ruins of Rye House are known as Rye House Castle, whilst 'Rye House' refers to the industrial estate which included Nissen's factory. The nearby suburb is called Rye Park, a ward of the town of Hoddesdon. A little muddling, perhaps ?

The mortgaged fields at Rye House and their former owners were:-

Mrs C Kingsley 3 acres
Emily Skipp 2 acres, with gravel pit
S A Fiske 2 acres
Emily Skipp 3 roods, 16 perches at Clappers Hook

In October 1932 another field was mortgaged -

Emily Skipp 2 acres, 1 rood, 24 perches at Marsh Furlong

NISSEN-PETREN PARLOUR HOUSE.

SCALE OF FEET

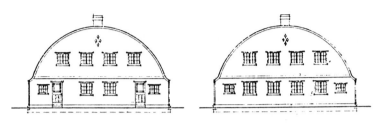

Front Elevation.   **Back Elevation.**

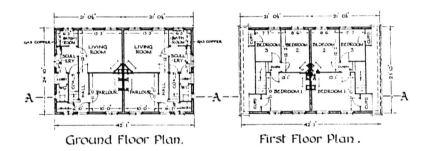

Ground Floor Plan.   **First Floor Plan.**

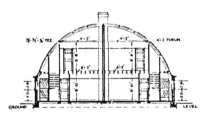 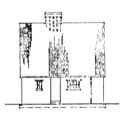

Section A-A.   **End Elevation.**

from *Nissen-Petren Houses.* The solution of the HOUSING PROBLEM.
(Nissen-Petren Houses Ltd, 75b Queen Victoria Street, London. printed by Stephen Murray & Co
Ltd, Yeovil.
(courtesy of Schreiber Furniture Ltd. From the collection of P.C.M. Nissen.)

119

The illustration shows a Nissen building in the factory of Messrs. Ericsson Telephones Ltd.

The obvious answer to the demand for **EMERGENCY ACCOMMODATION!**

Those manufacturers who are considering the erection of an emergency factory in the country should, in their own interests, consider the advantages of the Nissen method of construction.

LIGHT, AIRY WORKING CONDITIONS *assist efficient working. Very many factories where precision work to fine limits is essential use Nissen buildings.*

EASY ERECTION—EASY EXTENSIONS. *Nissen buildings are easy to erect and, by virtue of their special construction, can always be extended with the minimum of alteration.*

LOW FIRST COST — LOW MAINTENANCE COSTS. *Nissen buildings can be erected for a fraction of the cost of conventional construction—and have proved themselves to be exceptionally inexpensive in maintenance.*

Plans and suggestions for all schemes of factory construction are always available. In addition to this work Nissen Buildings Ltd. are specialists in the construction of Air Raid Shelters, Control Rooms, First-Aid and Decontamination Stations, buildings for the storage of A.R.P. equipment, etc., etc.

The

NISSEN

METHOD OF CONSTRUCTION
Nissen Buildings Limited,
Rye House, Hoddesdon, Hertfordshire.
Telephone: Hoddesdon 3001/2/3.

An advertisement from *The Financial Times* of June 2nd 1939.

(courtesy of Schreiber Furniture Ltd. From the collection of P.C.M. Nissen.)

Bless you ! Spirit of Emily Skipp ! You retained the medieval field names as seen in the tithe maps of about 1840, even though the ruins of a disused factory now covers them. To complete the purchase it was necessary to raise nine debentures of £250 each, of which one of the mortgagees was Walter Chamberlain, who was now the solicitor to Nissen's Ltd. Another was Captain William Henry Folkes, Managing Director of Nissen's Ltd, who had served in the Royal Engineers during the war with his friend Captain George Cox MBE who also joined the company.

Tragedy struck in 1923. Nissen had been living alone in Twickenham, London, whilst Louisa remained with family in California. The Secretary of the Institute of Mining and Metallurgy in London, Mr E C McDermid, had a house, 'Deepdale', built for him in 1910, about halfway up Westerham Hill, in Kent. On visiting the house Nissen had greatly admired the view down the vale, called Holmesdale and, as the house was for sale, he bought it in 1922, in time to welcome Louisa back home from overseas. Nissen's choice of future home is not surprising; returning from south east London, by car today one feels, on descending Westerham Hill, over the North Downs, that you are entering genuine countryside, leaving behind the concrete and brick culture of Greater London.

To 'Deepdale' returned a desperately ill Louisa, who died in a Nursing Home in July 1923 at the age of 50, from bronchopneumonia and femoral thrombosis.

The aim to provide residential housing of Nissen Hut design required some modification and thus two-storey houses were designed by Messrs Petter & Warren, architects to the Yeovil Borough Council in Somerset. They were to be built by Nissen's Ltd, which now included Robert Donger as Chief draughtsman. Demobilised from the Royal Engineers in 1919 as a Sergeant, he was employed for a short period by an engineering firm in Victoria Street, London until 1921 when he joined Nissen's Ltd and remained with them until his untimely death in 1952 at the early age of 60, weakened by Paget's disease.

The Nissen-Petren houses, as they were called, were marketed by a separate company, Nissen-Petren Houses Ltd of London, of which Nissen was one of the directors and which acted as a public relations link between customer and manufacturer. Two such semi-detached houses were built in 1925 in Yeovil with corrugated asbestos-steel roofs, supported by a framework of semicircular steel ribs. Little notice appears to have been taken of them until early 1983 when, as a result of an application from the Somerset County Council, they were listed as Grade II houses of architectural and historical interest. Further, the Somerset County Council thought the two houses "an important example of an experimental cost-cutting design, aimed at producing cheap housing between the wars. Our concern is not with the interior or its convenience as a home, but with its historical or architectural role in the community."

This was in reply to the Yeovil Borough Council's wish to demolish the houses which could only be carried out if the Ministry of the Environment would lift the listing order. "The bureaucrats in London accepted the recommendation automatically. If they had seen it they would have had it pulled down as a monstrosity. We have appealed." said the Borough Council, "and hope it can be lifted." But the protest failed. More enthusiasm for Nissen-Petren houses was displayed by the Yeovil Rural District Council which built 22 of them at the villages of South Petherton, Barwick and West Camel, but the council soon reverted to the traditional type of house. Eight of these houses can be seen from the A303 at West Camel.

Surprisingly, an element of class distinction is perceived in the limited choice of house plans by Nissen-Petren, as they were referred to as the 'Parlour House' and the 'Non-Parlour House' ! For it was still the age when the parlour was for Sunday use only, where family and friends could 'parley', or chat, but beyond this social function the parlour was a status symbol. I recollect that in 1932, I lodged as a bachelor in a Council house which lacked a bathroom, but enjoyed Sunday afternoon tea in the parlour ! The main difference between the two plans was that a third bedroom in the Non-Parlour house replaced, on the ground floor, the parlour of the other plan; a parlour was sacrificed for increased space in the three bedrooms. Both house types had a scullery, bathroom, lavatory and something which is sadly missing in houses built today - a larder ! Undoubtedly a revolutionary type of residence in that the asbestos protected metal roof was not supported by walls, but by metal ribs bolted to the foundation concrete.

122

For a document intended to sell these houses, the publication *Nissen-Petren Houses - the solution of the housing problem,* is a brochure prepared with great care, briefly mentioning the essential points likely to be raised by a potential buyer, the whole prefaced by those nostalgically yearning lines of Padraic Colum's 'An old woman of the roads',

'And am I praying to God on high,
And am I praying Him night and Day,
For a little house -a house of my own -
Out of wind's and the rain's way.'

Yet, in spite of the rancour which arose from the listing of the Yeovil houses the credit is with the Yeovil Borough Council which was tackling locally the national problem of housing thousands of people without any houses on offer and of Councils without finance to built them. Yeovil had about 600 applicants of whom more than 400 were lodged in overcrowded quarters. Yeovil thought that the Nissen-Petren houses at a cost of £350 was the answer, but lost their initial enthusiasm when it was found that they cost, in the end, £100 more than the traditional house and so the original plan of building more Nissen-Petren houses was abandoned.

The commercial and industrial boom, usually associated with the end of a war, had now faded into a recession, but a mini war in North Africa secured a contract for Nissen Huts to be supplied to the army in Spanish Morocco for the military campaign against a leader of the indigenous peoples, Ab-del-Krim, in the Rif mountains (1921-26). Worthy of note is the dust storm of 1925 that levelled everything except the Nissen Huts which were left standing!

A medical practitioner once gave me his opinion that of all the medical discoveries of the twentieth century he would rank antibiotics among the best. Had they been discovered earlier than 1929, when penicillin was isolated, there would have been a vastly different interlude in this biography. Walter Chamberlain returned home towards the end of December 1929 with a 'chill' and died early in January, at the age of 60. The vast concourse that attended his funeral service in Croydon included Nissen. Four weeks later, Nissen returned home from Hoddesdon, also with a 'chill' but in spite of the attention of two doctors and expert nursing he died on March 2nd 1930, when pneumonia supervened, as was the same with Chamberlain. Two men, in their prime, for Nissen was only 58. Again, a large number of mourners, first the coffin escorts which included Capt 'Bill' Folkes, Robert Donger and Charles Fletcher, who was one of the mortgagees of the original fields at Rye House. Other Hoddesdon folk there were Harold John (a director), Donald Henderson (secretary) and John Payne (chauffeur to Folkes). The staff and workmen at Hoddesdon sent a floral tribute.

The keystone had dropped out of the arch, but the building had remained firm. Nissen's premature death could never have meant the closing of Nissen's Buildings. Although insufficiently financed, it lumbered on under the impetus of originality and invention. If official company certificates proclaimed the methods of avoiding bankruptcy by a succession of share issues, the evidence is seen more dramatically in a letter to me from an employee of those days:

"I know that it was difficult to pay the wages sometimes. Telephone calls were exchanged between Leabank Chair Co., Concrete Utilities and others to obtain short term loans when cheques had not been received from customers The company held a small amount of steel in stock together with some timber and a whole variety of fittings, rivets, bolts and nuts, sheet fittings and so on. Almost everything worked on what is now called 'just in time'. If it was in the factory, it was for a job. Materials to be delivered to a site were called for as needed. Everyone was paid when the job was finished and the final cheque received."

After five years, two mortgages and an issue of one thousand shares, a liquidator was called in. Percy Edgar Slack of Silversides, Slack and Barnby, incorporated accountants of 44 Bedford Row, London WC1. His drastic recommendations to Nissen included the closing of the London Office, thus saving the salaries of Messrs Webb and Cox and buying up the firm, by paying back the debenture holders, which was now possible with funds from the family of his new wife, Lauretta Maitland, having remarried in 1924. After which Nissen's Ltd became registered as Nissen Buildings Ltd.

As might be expected, 1930 was a watershed in the history of Nissen Buildings. It had started in countryside, on the banks of the river Lea, continues my informant, who joined Nissen Buildings Ltd in 1935. "So with river navigation, railway connection and road access, Nissen's had the classic late 19th century, early 20th century industrial site." He describes the

124

situation:-

"Nissen's occupied a site by the river Lea, on the west bank almost opposite the pleasure garden, that were once part of the attractions that went with the old Rye House Castle. Lawns, statues, with and without heads, peacocks, a sports ground used for athletic meetings, boats for hire, a big pub and a dance hall."

"A tall black corrugated iron fence, curving round along the edge of the tow path, marked the eastern end of the site. A pot-holed gravel road connected the Rye House road with the factory. The northern side had a hawthorn hedge, separating the factory site from Fiske's farm. Fiske was an Irishman, running a small farm with his wife and family. I remember the goats, a few pigs, chickens and horses. Along the western side ran the Great Eastern section of the London and North Eastern Railway, with Rye House Station and a goods section, which was linked to Nissen's Buildings yard. The fourth side linked the railway boundary to the towpath along the river. A hawthorn hedge separated the rough ground near the railway from the Nissen's Sports Club cricket ground; some more rough ground, then the bungalow where Mr Donger and his family lived. On the factory side of the hedge was a pond. This was the result of earlier gravel excavations which had filled with water. The pond was slowly being filled in as it was available as a tip for hardcore (old broken bricks). At the railway end the pond was being filled with sawdust and shavings from the woodshop. As we walked across it to the cricket field the damp sawdust bounced under our weight.... Nissen's were making great efforts to sell a large part of the site for industrial development. It was necessary for the drawing office to erase the words 'SUBJECT TO FLOODS' from the Ordnance Survey maps they held ! Addis Ltd had a board advertising their toothbrushes, erected facing the Cambridge-Liverpool Street railway line. ....Two Nissen buildings, each about 40 feet span, ran along the Northern hedge for about 120 feet. The materials for these buildings, I was told by the woodshop foreman, David Willetts, was surplus from the National Wool Sheds, that had been erected by the company at Hull. Most of the machinery in the factory was pre-World War I. This part of the factory produced all the timber parts for the buildings, purlins, bearers, end framing, doors, windows and so on...."

"Parallel with these was the steel shop. Two bays about 35 feet span, some 12 feet to eaves with orthodox steel trusses. This also had old machinery dating back to the beginning of the century. The floor was earth with the machines in concrete foundations. There were rails let into the runs of

125

The Donger family residence at Rye House, Hoddesdon, a Nissen hut with verandah added, giving it a colonial appearance. Robert Donger stands at the entrance whilst his wife is near the french doors.
(courtesy of Mr Ken Willetts.)

concrete to feed work to the machines and a floor above one area where template, or pattern making was done. In this shop were made all the steel parts for the buildings, with a smaller area adjoining for sheet metal work. Also on site was a small office, used by Jewsons, to manage the timber that was delivered to them by barge. This was unloaded and stacked by hand. Some part of the site was used for the storage of the rough cut timber.

There were a few small buildings on the site, that closest to the factory was the engine house. This was a gas engine, looked after by Alfred (Uncle) Pridiss. The fuel used was anthracite and the whole machine was an enormous problem to start in the winter. As it provided direct current power to the factory and for lighting the site, it was essential to get it started. A gang from the factory had to heave on the long driving belt to get the thing turning. It took a number of heaves, before there was a great 'chuff', and the engine began to chuff away without further help."

Were the trade employees all journeymen - those who had learnt their trade as apprentices ? No reference is made to the number of apprentices employed by Nissen Buildings, with one exception, My informant began there as an office boy and became a draughtsman, which suggests that there was a form of training in at least one trade. But as office boy he contributes a lively account of a day in his life:-

"My duties were to sweep out, clean and dust three offices each morning. The first office was that of Mr W H Folkes, managing director, the second that of Mr D B Henderson, the company secretary. The third one was the general office, staffed by the clerk, Mr R S Porter, another junior clerk, Mr V H Brown, a typist, Mrs A Bugg and finally, in the corner, the office boy. After sweeping out the offices, I had to light two fires during the cold weather. The wood for kindling the fires came from the wood shop, which was run by Mr David Willetts, then fill the buckets with coal and, during the day, be certain that Mr Folkes's fire did not go out. Finally, I cleaned the toilets ! At 9.00 am, the staff arrived and my day's work began. The switchboard was mine with its two incoming lines and five extension lines, which included one for the drawing office, where Mr R Donger presided over four or five draughtsmen. I also had to keep records of the stock issued by Mr R E Cook of the stores, separate the items into types, record the types for each job going through the factory and produce a cost sheet for them"

Maurice Fox, for that is his name, had the makings of James Barrie's 'Admirable Crichton', or to use a more modern example, the BBC's 'Jim'll Fix It' !

A factory in the midst of unspoilt country perhaps, but Nissen Buildings could not fit the title of 'an island entire in itself'. The feeling of extended family among the staff and workers did not encourage the growth, as it might have done, of a tightly knit clique; instead there was a sense of kindred. David Willetts has been mentioned as foreman of the workshop. Reading his obituary notice of 1962 in the *Hertfordshire Mercury*:-

'Mr Willetts was a trustee of the Hoddesdon Methodist Church, to which he gave practical support in many ways. Both the original building and the subsequent extension, of the Wesley Hall, owed a great deal to his knowledge and help and both hall and church bear, besides, many evidences of his skilful workmanship. He had the present wall entrance gate outside the church built in the memory of his eldest son, David, who died on military service in 1940. Mr Willetts was keenly interested in both football and cricket. He was a former committee member of Hoddesdon Town Football Club."

Captain 'Bill' Folkes set an example in community co-operation with active interests in the local branch of the British Legion, in the Angling Society and in the local football and cricket. As early as 1937, he was planning air raid shelters based on underground Nissen huts. His daughter Katherine was manageress of the canteen at the Nissen Sports and Social Club which, from local press reports, was a popular and thriving leisure organisation. Another employee worthy of mention was Victor King, who worked at the Nissen Canteen and was responsible for First Aid management. Not so unusual perhaps ? For he had previously worked at the Hedley Pit in Durham county and for his rescue work at a pit disaster he was awarded the King George V medal and received a Carnegie Hero fund award.

The sense of family included not only 'Bill' Folkes, David Willetts, Victor King, Robert Donger and Stanley Pridiss, but extended to Charlie Miles, foreman of the metal shop, Jack Payne, the driver, Donald Henderson, the book-keeper (later, the company secretary) and Mrs Kenton, the caretaker who lived in a Nissen hut in her garden, where she cared for her hens and her roses - all pleasantly living out their days when production standards were

128

equal to, if not superior to financial considerations, before national and global entrepreneurs had rendered the world a very small place indeed.

Yet for all this pleasantry, there were the hidden antagonisms prevalent in the Hoddesdon district, which frequently arose in a self-organised fashion of which the main sparring bodies were, firstly, Rye Park residents versus Hoddesdon Council and, secondly, Rye Park residents versus local industry of which Nissen Buildings was a prime target. It was a familiar 'not in my back yard' or NIMBY attitude. Of course, these two forms of antagonism were often related and sometimes it was almost Rye Park versus the world, or at least the world of small-town politics. The main attacking front was a perpetual demand that the Rye Park ward of the Council should have a larger representation, a plea that was repeatedly ignored by Hoddesdon Council, since only one third of Rye Park electors ever troubled to cast their votes in Council elections. There was a spark of humour, when a Rye Park resident, an obvious admirer of Burns, published in the *Hoddesdon Journal* of March 1949, a poem from an unnamed local paper in January 1887, to prove that environmental conditions had not improved:-

'Can a body see a body
At night time on the Rye ?
There is no light, there is no gas
And yet the rates are high
And if a body can't afford
To have a bus or fly
He's sure to stick deep in the mud
When coming from the Rye'

We can assume that in 1887 the bus or fly was truly horse-powered.

The previous list of small holdings mortgaged by Nissen in 1922, hardly represent the total, because on 13th April 1934 *The Herts Mercury* announced, 'Factory sites at Rye Park, Hoddesdon... Apply Nissen Buildings Ltd, Rye House.' Some 27 acres were for sale. Hoddesdon Council found it necessary to warn prospective buyers that two difficulties were to be overcome, the disposing of waste water and the supply of clean or drinking water. From press reports and those of the Housing and Town Planning Committee of the Hoddesdon Council, it appears that the Council was sympathetic towards Nissan Building planning applications, but emphasising the disposal of waste water and the provision of clean water. The building sites were fraught with such difficulties. Conservation clashed with safety in one Nissen application for a factory extension in Hoddesdon, where the Council insisted on an increase in the number of fire exits and the removal of an existing building which had a thatched roof.

Although the local press took little notice of the feuds between Rye Park residents and the Council or Industry, sensing perhaps that such fueds were of little interest to their readers, the monthly *Hoddesdon Journal* published a complaint about the unsuitability of the Nissen built Widbury Press, together with a photograph of what appears to be a pleasant building. Too near the river, may be, as if it were about to be launched, but its importance had been escalated by appearing in the *Illustrated London News.* "What do our readers think about it ?" asked the Journal, in a caption to the photograph. A daily newspaper could hardly hold the attention of its readers for more than three days on such a subject and so we are not surprised to find only one letter on the Widbury Press in the following month's issue and that merely complained about a promised tree screen between the Press and the river which had yet to be planted !

The inventive ingenuity of Nissen knew no bounds. There being no further call for his Nissen Steel Tent, he remodelled it minus the corrugated iron wall. Once erected, the wall was constructed locally, with stone, or sun-dried brick, known as adobe, or 'Kimberley' brick. But who required them ? Living in Westerham, was General Sir John Asser, who had spent part of his career in the Sudan and believed that such a hut would be suited to house the Arab workers on the cotton plantations. The 'Tukl', as it was marketed, was discontinued as the plantations, themselves, were not a financial success. But some had been exported to the Sudan, which accounts for the advertisement. Chainstore owner, Aziz Kfouri, almost certainly Greek, had branches in Khartoum, Port Sudan, Omdurman and Medani. He advertised in Greek, because the storekeepers, or most of them, were descended from Egyptian Greeks, who in the course of time had started stores in most African countries.

130

AZIZ KFOURI

Καλύβαι ἐκ χάλυβος, προνομιούχου συστήματος Nissen, ἰδεώδεις διὰ τὰς ἐπαρχίας καὶ ἁπλούσταται. Στήνονται εἰς 3 ὥρας μόνον καὶ λύονται εἰς τὸ ἥμισυ τοῦ χρόνου τούτου. Παρακολουθήσατε μίαν δοκιμήν. Μία εἶνε στημένη εἰς τὰς ἀποθήκας μας

The Tukl. Aziz Kfouri advertises huts (Tukls) for sale at his four branches in the Sudan. *There is a translation in the text, but the newspaper is unknown.* (From the collection of P.C.M. Nissen.)

131

The advertisement reads as follows:-

'Iron huts, a privileged (sic, prestigious ?) production of Nissen.
Ideal for the countryside, very simple
Put up in only three hours. Taken down in half the time
Attend a demonstration
One erected in our showroom.'

'Tukl' does not appear in an Arabic dictionary, but there is 'Tqeel' meaning 'something heavy', which was possibly the reaction of Kfouri's labourers, when erecting the 'tent' and then dismantling it during demonstrations ! The 'Tukl' may have been derived from the 'Nissen Steel tent', but there were differences, which allowed for the sub-tropical climate in which they were required. The steel ceiling supported a three inch layer of mud, without which the temperature inside the hut would have been insufferable. There was also a circle of mosquito gauze below the cowl for huts in malarial districts. No doubt, the erection of a Tukl and its subsequent dismantling provided the local population with four and a half hours non-stop commentary of the facetious kind.

Manufacture of the Tukl parts is described by a *Hertfordshire Mercury* reporter, visiting the Rye House factory in May 1933. Here are the main points of his write-up:-

"And speaking of the Tukl - we examined one of the buildings, made specially to serve the Eastern market. A corrugated steel door bolts onto uprights and, after the roof sheets have been fixed, the circular frame can be filled in with suitable local material to form the walls. At the same time, there are special fitments for the door and windows covered with bronze netting to keep out the flies.....Nissen's send abroad the various buildings in sections, which unskilled men can assemble with the ease that a child constructs models. The sections are easily packed, shipped and handled without difficulty. In the steel shed at Rye House, men were busy cutting and drilling stanchions (uprights) and purlins (horizontals).... The principal skilled worker was engaged in making templates, or patterns, used as a guide for shaping the steel to exact requirements. Heavy steel bars were fed into machines and cut to the necessary lengths and shapes in a few seconds. The main object was accuracy, so that each part of the structure could be built up and re-erected without any question of misfits. Obviously, a tea planter in Ceylon would be very annoyed if he had to cable the factory, because his native workers were stuck in the work of the erection. .... In addition to the steel shop at Rye house, there is also a large joinery works. Every kind of fitting required is made in the factory. .... The whole of the land in the vicinity is marked out for industrial development and is self contained for all purposes, including the provision of a railway siding. It is a hive of industry, with lorries passing to and fro; steel and timber being unloaded from barges; circular saws constantly humming; men hammering; forges glowing; and that steady insistent note of industrial activity which is the heartbeat of the machine."

Truly a vivid picture of a minor industrial revolution, in an age of innocence !

Although the Tukl appeared to have the qualities of a hut suited to the tropics, it was the Nissen hut that continued to be the more favoured seller, if only a sideline compared with the numerous industrial types which left the Rye House factory. The *Hertfordshire Mercury* reporter continues with more interesting facts about Nissen's Buildings:-

"As we called the other day upon Mr W H Folkes, managing director of Nissen Buildings Ltd, conversation carried across continents in a few minutes. It was not long before Mr Folkes was standing before a map of the world and we felt the heat of the tropics as he described desert scenes and produced photographs, showing actual places where buildings from Rye House are now housing .... maybe native chiefs with goodness knows how many wives !" (Although not mentioned, each wife would have a separate hut! Nowhere in the world do women share kitchens pleasantly !)

"To watch the Nissen buildings made and see how easily they can be assembled is to appreciate the simplicity of solving the housing problem where primitive conditions preclude restrictions associated with building bye laws.... Today, the shops at Rye House turn out all kinds of constructional steelwork; steel frame buildings from 16 feet to 50 feet span. The hut is, more or less, a sideline, which, however, has proved adaptable for use in the remote parts of Europe, Africa and Asia. For example, the work of damming the river Nile, meant providing quarters for native labour and the Nissen hut proved a clean and cool building, which could be kept far more sanitary than mud dwellings used by the local natives. Actually, the reeds which thatched the native huts before Nissen arrived were brought 600 miles. (Surely an exaggeration ?) There have been calls for these huts from the Sudan, South

133

Africa and Kenya. An oil company in Iraq purchased hundreds and the home market is not yet satisfied. Nissen huts are at present being erected in Labour Training Camps."

Factories and houses were not the only examples of Nissen type buildings. There were several churches and the Church of the Holy Angels at Cranford, Middlesex was one of them. Built in 1935 to cope with increasing numbers of worshippers, it was decided to have a Nissen hut. I was drafting this paragraph, when I found a newspaper photograph of the church exterior. Depressed by the drabness of the scene I continued writing with the superficiality of some 'tabloid' reporter. "When dedicated by the Bishop of Kensington, he declared that it was 'a modern church for modern people.' A clichéd remark, which I would dispute on viewing the photograph of what is an enlarged Nissen hut, wholly functional, but neither aesthetic nor divinely inspiring." I have had to 'eat my words' since receiving a packet of press cuttings and photographs, not only about this dedication service in 1935, but another such service in 1941, because the 1935 church was burnt down, arson being suspected. Yet the congregation wanted nothing less, or more, than another Nissen hut. The managing director of Nissen Buildings, Capt W H Folkes was present at this second dedication in 1941, when the press notice not only records his gift of £40, a considerable sum at that date, but also noted that Nissen Buildings executed the exterior and interior painting without charge. This second Nissen church was burnt down in 1969, but this time it was replaced with 'a lofty box building, with a large hall built in the High Street'. Perhaps aesthetic tastes had changed, or that Nissen Buildings were no longer in the building trade, but had changed to the manufacture of television and radio cabinets, under the influence of one of the new directors, Chaim Schreiber.

From an artistic and technical angle, the outstanding example of Nissen hut conversion must have been the Italian chapel on the Orkney island of Lambholm, where several hundred Italian prisoners of war were housed in camp 60, during the Second World War of 1939-45. Captured during the North African campaign, they were employed to construct the Churchill barrier, a series of concrete causeways, which sealed the Eastern approaches to that huge natural harbour of the Orkneys, Scapa Flow. Most of these approaches had been sealed in 1918, when the defeated German fleet scuttled

Holy Angels Church, Cranford, which is very like a cinema.

THE SUNDAY REFEREE. 5

1-3-36.

Britain's Strangest Church Looks Like a Cinema

TIP-UP CHAIRS, RADIO, LOUD-SPEAKERS— AND NO SERMONS!

(courtesy of the *News of the World*) (From the collection of Mr Eric Beales, Hounslow.)

135

The Italian chapel at Lambholm, Orkney (from *Orkney's Italian Chapel*, The Orcadian Press.) (courtesy of John A Muir Esq. Treasurer, Italian (Prisoners of War) Chapel Preservation Committee.

Hoddesdon Journal

OF DIRECT INTEREST TO EVERY HODDESDON FAMILY

PUBLISHED MONTHLY **CIRCULATION 5,000**

Vol. 5 OCTOBER, 1939 No. 10

"Why are them Nissen Huts built that shape?"

"So as yer can't get yerself in a tight corner, fathead!"

Nissen Buildings Limited, Rye House, Hoddesdon

Reproduced from "Punch"

The Hoddesdon Journal attributes this cartoon to *Punch*, but its origin is unknown. The '*Punch*' Library denies that it is one of theirs. (From the collection of P.C.M. NIssen.)

NAAFI GOT ONLY BATH

THIRTY-FIVE officers at an Army camp were supplied with two foot shower-baths, according to War Office schedule. But next door the N.A.A.F.I. manager, who was a civilian, was allowed a "sort of glorified flat" which included a full-length bath.

This story was told in the House of Commons yesterday, during the debate on the Address, by Capt. Profumo (Con., Kettering).

"I cannot imagine," he commented, "why the N.A.A.F.I. manager could not wash in the same bath as his Majesty's officers."

He went on to tell of another Army camp which was not completed when the unit moved in about a fortnight ago.

This camp was found to contain several old wooden Army huts, well constructed, which had been used before the war and were now occupied by the workers on the camp.

Strike Threat

The commanding officer considered it would be beneficial to put his men in some of these huts, where they could be accommodated side by side. It would make administration easier.

The clerk of works was delighted to consent to this, but he came back a few minutes later to say that the workmen said if they were moved out of the huts they would strike.

The workmen placarded the camp with notices, "No Nissen stys for the workers."

The commanding officer stuck to his orders. Half an hour later a high official arrived and told him the matter must be hushed up immediately or it would jeopardise the building of all the other camps in the division, many of which were not completed.

Capt. Profumo suggested that Mr. Bevin was not living up to his reputation and the Ministry of Labour did not take strong enough action about disputes of this kind.

NISSEN STIES ! A poor press for the hut ? From the *Daily Mail* of Nov 14th 1941. A NAAFI canteen is run by the Navy, Army and Air Force Institute. Ernest Bevin was Minister of Labour in Churchill's Government. (From the collection of P.C.M. Nissen.)

138

their battleships, on arriving at Scapa Flow. But in 1939, a German U-boat commander, aided by a high tide, entered Scapa Flow and torpedoed the battleship *Royal Oak*, which sank with the loss of over 800 men. Apart from the Churchill barrier, the Italians made concrete paths around their thirteen huts and planted flowers. One was an artist with a flair for organisation - Domenico Chiocchetti - who sought out the craftsmen among the prisoners, cement workers, smiths in iron and brass, and electricians. Together, they connected two Nissen huts into a chapel with simple materials, mostly second hand; even the artistic candlesticks were fashioned out of old corned beef tins ! First the sanctuary was completed, with altar, altar rail and holy water stoup, all moulded in concrete, to which was added a wrought iron sanctuary screen. This gorgeous conversion emphasised the drabness of the hut walls, so they were painted by Chiocchetti and an assistant to represent brickwork. But that left the depressing exterior, which was then hidden by a cement facade. Eventually, it became a place of pilgrimage, attracting thousands of tourists, whose donations provide the materials for the preservation of the chapel, in an unfriendly climate. Many such tourists are truly pilgrims and among them we count Domenico Chiocchetti, who has occasionally returned to repair the art work. The Treasurer of the Italian (Prisoners of War) Chapel Preservation Committee, John Muir, provides some interesting information:-

"I had never given any consideration as to why the Nissen hut was so called and certainly never connected it with the name of the 'inventor'. During the war, the whole of the Orkney Islands had Nissen huts dotted all over the place and, indeed, there are still some surviving on farms, being used for storage of implements etc., Of course, the Nissen rated most highly is the Chapel and I am sure it must be the most visited Nissen in the whole country, with sixty five thousand visitors last year. The artist who created the chapel, Domenico Chiocchetti, is still alive (85 years old) and living in Moena, in Northern Italy and I had the great pleasure of visiting the family last September, when I attended the annual reunion of the ex-prisoners from the Orkney camps, which was held in Vinci, near Florence." The letter was dated 22nd January 1996.

The contrasted reactions of the two congregations to Nissen hut churches are interesting. Holy Angels wished the hut to be visible, whereas the Italians concealed it behind a concrete facade. Perhaps we are comparing 'a modern church for modern people', with a traditional church for a traditional culture ?

139

Among a bunch of undated pages torn from magazines of unknown origin I found the following extracts, obviously written during the first and 'phoney' period of the Second World War:-

"There is little need for us to tell the old soldier of the origin of the Nissen hut and its usefulness in *his* war. Before the Great War finished, every theatre of war had its complement of the ubiquitous Nissen huts - some titivated up and named 'The Ritz', 'Savoy' or 'Berkeley' - others more proletarian named 'The Better 'Ole' or perhaps 'Sea View' - but all of them serving their purpose of giving warm dry shelter to men who prized this above all other comfort. .... Peace came and the man at arms returned to his suburban villa, cottage or his ancestral mansion and the memory of the Nissen hut faded with other reminders of active service."

"Then the wheel turned full circle and, unhappily, we were forced once more to take up arms. Many things were different this time, however. There was no immediate shattering offensive, no hasty improvisations. .... Britain goes to war in a different way, yet with the same spirit. One link at last, holds two generations together. On the battlefields of Europe stand the Nissen huts. New, better Nissen huts perhaps., but still there for the same purpose of giving comfortable living conditions for the soldiers of Britain. The veteran of the last war, who is serving again with the British Expeditionary Force will find his Nissen hut more roomy, more commodious, but the old familiar construction will awaken many lingering memories of the other great conflict in France and, perhaps, memories of old friends and comrades in arms, who shared his life in a Nissen hut so many years ago."

That was before the Allied retreat from Dunkirk from May 29th to June 4th 1940. If there were a more stringent test of a Nissen hut it would be difficult to find one more taxing that that experienced by the 'Tingloos', of Iceland during the 1939-45 War, when the United States forces were accommodated in what they regarded as 'tin-igloos', disappointed though they were on discovering that Eskimos and polar bears, did not exist in Iceland ! From the standpoint of morale, theirs was a difficult task. Trained to grapple with the enemy on the mainland of Europe, they found that they had occupied an environmentally inhospitable island, which they did not want, with a population that needed no protection, for they were there to protect the sea routes between North America and Europe. Iceland in the hands of the Nazis would have meant that U-boats plying from the fiords of that country would have had absolute control over these sea routes. The strangeness of a new land

140

was tempered by the irritating fact that there was little hope of seeking the enemy, as one soldier complained; "When my grandchildren ask me, forty years from now, what I did in the war, it will sure be humiliating to tell them that I sat in a Nissen hut and guarded an extinct volcano." Social opportunities to know the young women were limited by a difficult language, but more so by the presence of a highly moral Lutheran society. As usual, the women, more innovative than the men, conversed in 'film American', rather than the text book English of their schools.

Under the more relaxed, if warlike, conditions of Iceland the troops commented favourably on their living conditions in Nissen huts, which by that time had developed into quarters superior to those built at Hesdin in France during the 1914-18 War. Some were now built on a concrete base and were provided with paraffin stoves in a country devoid of trees. The huts were assembled in 'streets', wired both inside and out for electric lighting and each street provided with a washing and toilet hut. I had previously wondered why the 1914-18 history of the Nissen huts did not include a mention of such last named facilities. The reason, of course, was that this was the province of the Royal Army Medical Corps of the British Army. The huts in France may have been tested by rain, frost, snow and shrapnel, but an additional menace appeared in Iceland - gales of often more than 100 miles an hour, overturning a Nissen hut and finally demolishing it, stripping off the corrugated iron roofing from its steel ribs, piece by piece. Banks of earth on each side of the hut usually prevented destruction on this horrific scale.

'Worst we ever had was in January, when it rained bucketfuls and the wind hit one hundred and twenty nine miles an hour. We also blew into the Atlantic. Some Nissen huts blew away and we had to crawl around on our hands and knees, putting sandbags on the roofs to hold the others down. A captain was blown into a barbed wire barricade and it took two fellows to pull him out." Altogether, the U.S. Army expressed great satisfaction with the huts. 'They are snug enough for anybody .... Splotched with dazzle paint, a community the size of a country village is invisible from the air'.

Above. Permanent huts had cement-block end-walls. IWM 2102
Below. Offices at an RAOC Depot. Note that the design included dormer windows. H 28897

(Both photgraphs courtesy of Imperial War Museum)

The increased output expected of any factory committed to wartime production was certainly true of Nissen Buildings, which went ahead with the manufacture of hut components in 1939. When war was declared the British army had no huts whatsoever in stock, but Nissen Buildings at once allowed the manufacture of huts of their design, without demanding royalty payments thus giving the immediate go-ahead for the production of Bow Huts and Hospital Huts for the British Expeditionary Force. This is a suitable moment to compare the hutting of the 1914-18 war with that of the 1939-45 war. Huts on Iceland for the United States troops had the advantage of electric lighting, oil burning stoves and concrete floors. The original Nissen huts were constructed with floors and ends of timber, but a shortage of timber compelled the use of concrete floors and brick ends to the huts, where hutting was not required to be moved. Later in the war, steel was also in short supply and, therefore, substitutes were tried, such as roofs of asbestos, concrete or even plasterboard, but the asbestos and concrete roofs failed to stand up to rough handling and plasterboard was apt to leak. The normal Nissen hut was declared 'too good a hut', for storage purposes and so a substitute with tubular steel ribs was devised, but most of them put themselves out of service, by collapsing under the weight of snow in the hard winter of 1940-41. An important addition to the Nissen huts was the introduction of dormer windows which rendered them less portable, but more popular with those who used them. Towards the end of 1941, it was decided to produce an improved type of Nissen hut, retaining the semicircular design, but with a sturdier framework. The narrow 'T' shaped ribs of the original Nissen hut were replaced by substantial two inch tubular steel and were joined by seven inch diameter couplers, each coupler taking four bolts, in contrast to the small box clips of the Nissen hut. The wooden purlins were discarded in favour of one and a half inch angle iron. This was the 'Romney' hut, which measured 96 feet by 35 feet. Much larger than the Nissen Bow Hut, which was 27 feet by 16 feet, or even the Nissen Hospital Hut which was 60 feet by 20 feet. I have not included the dimensions of the 'T' shaped ribs or the box clips as they were manufactured from whatever steel was available at the time. The 'Romney' was the hut in general use during the campaigns in the North African desert.

The war was now over, but the leaders had gone. First Chamberlain and Nissen in 1930, then Folkes in 1944. A house-building department was established and a structural steelwork shop started. If the steelwork shop was a money spinner, this could not be said of house building. This was badly managed, but there were considerable problems with labour and the supply of materials. Nissen Buildings was opening a new housing estate at Dafen, near Llanelli, in South Wales, which depended upon supplies of corrugated iron from the Gorse Galvanising Company, of which John H John, a Nissen director, was also a director. Another example of double directorship was that of Harold Burn, whose firm supplied Nissen's with Vitreflex Patent Corrugated Strips, for securing the corrugated roofing sheets, without making holes in the sheets; Burn was a director of both Vitreflex and Nissen Buildings, but these attempts at co-operation did little to halt the downward slide of Nissen's toward eventual extinction.

Was it a challenge to the business world or a rescue operation ? On July 27th 1953, a resolution was passed at an Extraordinary Meeting of the Nissen Board and presumably all those who held shares and debentures, at the offices of Silverside, Slack and Barnby, at 44 Bedford Row, London WC1, with the object of changing the aims of the Company. This bizarre manifesto, covering several pages with sub-sections from (a) to (z) started thus:-

(a) To carry on in any part of the world, all or any of the businesses of builders, contractors, builders merchants, glaziers, joiners, carpenters, woodworkers, plasterers, painters, plumbers, shopfitters and cabinet makers, hydraulic, electrical, radio, radar, refrigeration. ventilation, sanitary, construction and general engineers. ....smiths, welders, carriers and cartage contractors.

And then:

(c) To carry on any other business of any description. .... or ancillary to the objects of the Company.

And finally:

(z) To amalgamate with any other Company whose objects are or include objects similar to those of this Company.

Perhaps the over emphasis on these ambitious aims was the source of two resolutions which, though commendable, led to the demise of Nissen Buildings. Firstly, to enter the television cabinet making industry and secondly, to raise the nominal capital of Nissen Buildings by £93,000, beyond the registered capital of £7,000, interdependent resolutions because of the necessity to raise new finance for the new trade of veneers. A Company report of 1955 shows how the 93,000 £1 shares were allotted, perhaps not so interesting to the reader, except that the names and occupations of the recipients display to me the continued influence of Peter Nissen, as three of them were directors in his day; Percy Edgar Slack, Herbert Overall Barnsley and Harold Septimus Burn. The manufacture of television cabinets was then an experimental trade as each factory was engaged in research and development on how to form veneers to fit television cabinets of various shapes. Nissen Buildings had a German employee, ex-prisoners of war, who had practised as a cabinet maker in Dresden, before the 1914-18 war. Eric Schade was developing a wood veneer bending process in which glued veneers were pressed into shape by electrical heating. Lack of sufficient finance limited the rate of progress achieved by Schade and in an increasingly competitive world, a better and quicker system had been evolved by Schreiber Furniture Ltd, which was working in collaboration with a German machinery manufacturer, Much of the work at Nissen Buildings was passed on to Schreiber at a time when it was generally considered that Nissen's had become insolvent. Following several unsuccessful attempts to sell the Rye House, Hoddesdon site and factory, it was bought in 1959 by Chaim Schreiber, to be worked in parallel with his furniture factory at Harlow in Essex, producing wood veneers for television and radio cabinets and fitted furniture for kitchens and bathrooms. Chaim Schreiber was born in 1918 in Poland and was training as an architect in Vienna when Hitler's troops invaded Austria at the time of the Anschluss, or annexation, of March 1938. As a Jew he fled the country. finding refuge in England, working in aircraft production during the 1939-45 War, after which he started a furniture factory at Stevenage, Herts and later his main factory and offices were at Edinburgh Way, Harlow.

After 1963, there appears to be a gradual transfer of activity from Hoddesdon to Harlow, under the name of Schreiber Furniture Ltd, with only three directors mentioned in the Company Reports, namely, Chaim Schreiber, his wife Sara and an architect, Ronald Eliason. This was truly the end of the Nissen story. The Companies Registration Office of the Department of Trade and Industry reported in 1977 that no Company Reports had been received for three years during which Nissen Steelwork was merely a name. The

Schreibers were granted three months grace to submit a report - ignored it - and in July 1977 the name Nissen Steelworks Ltd was removed from the list of Companies - 'Nissen's' was now officially dead ! The Hoddesdon site of 22 acres was sold in 1977 and is at present owned by the Ladbroke chain of hotels.

Although the lingering end of 'Nissen's' appears a sad anti-climax, it was, perhaps, inevitable in a new industrial world of mergers and their competitiveness, with emphasis on 'market value' and 'cost effectiveness', concepts which gave rise to a new breed of directors and managers, ambitious and dedicated. On looking back we note that the Nissen success depended upon building types based on the 'hut', which was rarely understood or appreciated in times of peace, however useful it was during the global wars of 1914-18 and 1939-45 and the Falklands campaign. This is no condemnation of Nissen houses in Somerset, but a vote of approval for the builders of modern conventional homes. The industrial period at Rye House, Hoddesdon, can be likened to a river, its source Nissen's Ltd, changing its name to Nissen Buildings Ltd, then Nissen's Steelworks Ltd and finally, losing itself in the Schreiber sands which were, in turn, engulfed in 1989 by the rising tide of MFI - financial advantage or poetic justice ?

146

7. NISSEN : MAN AND INVENTOR

So far, six uncomplicated chapters about Peter Norman Nissen, but this last chapter has proved the most difficult. Chapter after Chapter informs us, I hope, about his early education, his professional life, his difficulties in promoting the Stamp Mill, rebutting the criticisms of the Nissen Hut, and much of this is gleaned second hand from his wife Lauretta's valuable notes. That she sustained his ego was essential to one who tended to exhibit an aversion to criticism, which he overcame as regards the Stamp Mill in his "Reply to Discussion" in *The Journal of the Chemical, Metallurgical and Mining Society of South Africa* of March 1912, but in the case of the Nissen hut of 1916, criticism was not so well received and so a second hut and even a third was constructed, before the Royal Engineer officers were satisfied. Perhaps the lonely life of a prospector and mining engineer in the New World did not induce the necessity for group consensus, the collective view of his professional peers ? Again, there are those who maintain that the stresses of professional or working life should not intrude on home life, but we cannot overestimate the easing of such stresses by genuine sympathy from one's partner and this he certainly received from Lauretta. Regrettably, this picture of a couple, determined to make a success of their marriage, lasted only eight years.

What then, of his first marriage ? Following an engagement of about three years, his marriage to Louisa lasted 23 years, during which time they seem to have been separated by intervals of mining assignments and war. Healthwise, from the start, Louisa appears to have been unsuited for life in a gold-mining compound. Illness on a train journey from Kingston to Arizona

147

may have induced Nissen to settle her at the Californian coast, near his own parents, who had now retired. A brief period of togetherness occurred in England and South Africa, lasting about two years, during which time Louisa was unwell in Johannesburg. Whether or not she spent the 1914-18 war years in California or England is not recorded, but in 1923 he returned with her from California, she in a poor state of health, shortly after which she died. Sensibly, he remarried in the following year, to Lauretta Maitland who gave him a son and was in course of giving him another when he died. He must have contemplated a reasonably long and most satisfactory life, noting the development of his two sons and perhaps, others. Somehow, I find in this biography the elements of tragedy, the perverseness of a career distinguished by professional success, yet not without its sadness over which he had little control; and a genuine private life unfolding, the dawn of another vocation as an industrialist, snatched away by a bacterium ! Further contrast is between the extrovert Queen's University student and the magisterial character revealed by his postwar portraits, except for the photograph showing him modelling the memorial to the 150 members of the Institute of Mining and Metallurgy , who fell in the 1914-18 war, which I have chosen for the frontispiece. There, it seems, he is happy at creative work, having witnessed four destructive years.

The almost complete lack of letters to and from Nissen does not help the biographer in assessing the temperament of the man who, to those who did not know him, may appear rather a 'cardboard character' than the controversial personality, that he was. With no letters to help me, what of the newspaper obituaries ? When the morning paper arrives, how many turn, as I do, to the obituaries ? Not because of a morbid or macabre obsession, but for style and content they contain some of the best of the morning's writing. Many are gems of little essays in literary criticism, balancing praise with disapproval where necessary. It was not always so. Nissen's death occurred at a time when obituaries of notables in the daily press were lean affairs of about sixty to two hundred words. The 44 Nissen obituaries I have read leave the reader in some doubt whether he was born in Canada or the United States, or whether he was fifty eight or fifty nine, when he died. Yet another and highly subjective difficulty is our own personal assessment of 'Man' as 'Male possessed of Manliness' complicated by the ever changing stereotypes of 'Manliness', which today may imply an aggressive 'Macho' category into which Nissen certainly does not fit. What better plan, then, to sound those who knew him ?

148

Much of Chapter 2 includes descriptions of Nissen family life in North Carolina, taken from a long letter to Lauretta Nissen from Reid Jones, the NIssen's neighbour in Thomasville. He refers to Nissen as "....... one whom I was proud to call my friend .... he seemed to stand out above the others....." Better still is Robert Donger's account of a critical period in his own life, when stricken by a disease believed to be fatal. He was then in France as a mechanical draughtsman under Nissen:-

"My interest in events now, unfortunately, waned due to a mysterious illness which befell me. I was passed from one doctor to another and none was able to diagnose the trouble. The Colonel revealed many personal touches and suggested that his friend Col Faulkner, in charge of 29th Field Ambulance, should take me in charge and it puzzled him also. I proved to be a puzzle and was duly put to bed and fed on an ordinary diet for three or four days, until Col Faulkner made an examination on Sunday morning, after which I was allowed milk only.

Col Faulkner apparently sent a grave message to Col Nissen, for the next thing I knew was Col Nissen being ushered into the room and taking a seat by my bed. He informed me that I was a serious case and would be removed by ambulance to Etaples, on the next day and, when well enough, would be sent to Blighty (England). He was obviously very much distressed and I have never forgotten the revelations of that day. Neither will I forget his insistence that I should be seen by a competent authority, for it did transpire that I was in a serious condition and further delay in receiving proper attention would probably have had fatal results. I was not in pain and, therefore, was inclined to treat the matter lightly during the Colonel's visit and we conversed at length. I say 'at length' because words came from me haltingly, for breathing was difficult. The Colonel was appreciative for the assistance I had been able to give him in his many and varied schemes and expressed an earnest wish that events should form themselves so that I should be brought back to his staff. He worked hard to that end and got Col Faulkner to see me on a few occasions when I was at Etaples. I was taken into the most suitable hospital for the complaint (nephritis) where research work was being carried out. I made a good recovery and, after six weeks, by special arrangement was sent back to the C.R.E. (Commander, Royal Engineers). My return coincided with the advent of winter and the Colonel was, at once, solicitous about my comfort and arrangements were made to treat me as a delicate subject."

Such a tribute speaks for itself and needs, I suggest, no further comment ! And, again, from Robert Donger, in a letter of condolence to Lauretta Nissen:-

"Dear Mrs Nissen,

I was present with the men at the works when the sad news of our beloved chief's end came. We all experienced a sensation of numbness. His association with us at the works has made a lasting impression upon us and we know full well that we have lost a real and sincere friend. ..... It has comforted me to sense the feelings of our men and to realise in what reverence they held the Colonel and it is this tribute from simple honest fellows which I wish to convey to you, for I am fully conscious that they all wish you to know how strongly they feel for you. .....

As promptly as two days after the funeral, Lauretta Nissen wrote a 'Thank-you' letter 'To the employees of Nissen Buildings Ltd' for 'the beautiful wreath you placed on my husband's grave. Your remembrance of him has given me genuine pleasure. .... His conception of the responsibilities of an employer of labour was very definite. He believed that it was his duty to strain every nerve to keep men employed. You all know how difficult this has been in the long period of industrial depression following the war. I used, sometimes, to deplore the fact that we could do so little in support of the endless appeals for the sick and unfortunate. My husband would reply 'I think to give honest men, who are willing to work, the chance to keep their wives and children in independence, is even more useful than to contribute to a Hospital or Country Holiday Fund'......

Few would agree with such sentiments, today !

And, from his Deputy Engineer-in-Chief, Brigadier General William Andre Liddell, with whom he had a close contact during the War, to Lauretta Nissen:-
'....I had a great respect for his ingenuity and resource and also for his personal qualities, his happy temperament and friendliness.....' followed by Liddell's memoir in the Royal Engineers Journal of September 1930: '..Cheery and humorous, he was a most attractive personality. He brought into all his enterprises the enthusiasm and optimism of a boy, undeterred by occasional failures... !

150

Hobbies and recreations ? From previous chapters, one might suggest that these could be included in one word, 'inventions', although we recollect his early love of dancing and sketching about which nothing further is heard. At his last home, 'Deepdale', Westerham, we find an enthusiastic and knowledgeable breeder and judge of Welsh Terriers and Irish Terriers who was often seen at shows. Obituaries in canine journals such as *Our Dogs* paid tribute to his great interest in these two doggy breeds. Perhaps of more permanent worth was his interest in sculpture. Starting with his daughter Betty's plasticine, he developed a skill which produced several bronzes, the best of which was the 1914-18 war memorial to the 150 fallen members of the Institute of Mining and Metallurgy in London. Their function as Tunnellers was to lay mines in the path of the enemy about to advance and to defuse those which the enemy had planted. It was doubtful if there were a more dangerous occupation during the war ! The memorial, unveiled by Field Marshall Earl Haig on 21st of November 1921, consisted of a malachite base surmounted by a bronze tunnelling officer in thigh boots, ankle deep in Flanders mud, who is in the act of exploding a mine with an electric exploder on a pile of sandbags. Sometime after Nissen's death the memorial was stolen from the offices of the Institution of Mining and Metallurgy in London, but later replaced by a mediocre replica which bears little resemblance to photographs of the original. Nissen's sculpture of a golfer for the newly formed Tandridge Golf Club in Surrey, suffered the same fate in about 1922. He was a founder member of the club and although he did not distinguish himself as a golfer he enjoyed the game and the company it attracted. From the evidence of others, he appears to have been an all-round personality.

It was Thomas Alva Edison, whose name is associated with the invention of the electric lamp, the phonograph which was the forerunner of the gramophone, the Edison effect in a vacuum lamp which lead to the thermionic valve of pioneer radio days and many other inventions, who stated that: "Genius is ten percent inspiration and ninety percent perspiration." Replace 'genius' by 'invention' and Edison's pithy saying still applies and, of course, he would have known this as a result of his 1097 patents. He was the perpetual inventor, the professional inventor who must incessantly give birth to new ideas and to improve the inventions of others. Perhaps the catalogues of ingenious gift items which appear in the mail include the efforts of the perpetual inventor such as the solar powered alarm clock or the ten-year guaranteed light bulb. Contrasted are the one time inventors of whom we hear no further. Such was Humphrey Potter, a cock-boy on a mine where the water was extracted by a pump, worked by a Newcomen engine where water and steam were alternately supplied to the cylinder of the pumping engine. The supplies were regulated by a cock-boy, who turned the cocks, or taps, at the appropriate moment. It was said that Humphrey, keen to watch a cricket match, attached strings of the correct length from the cocks to the beam which joined the pump to the engine, and thus the pump worked automatically ! After which Humphrey Potter disappears from history. Between the extremes of Edison and Potter, a whole gamut of inventors, both great and small, each patenting their inventions with the aid of a patents agent. Nissen's first patent illustrates in a simple manner, the outline of a patent application. The family home was in Halifax, Nova Scotia, but a local engineering firm had sent him to Queen's University, Kingston, Ontario. Oddly, the patent had little to do with either mining or huts, but it might have been useful to a mining prospector tramping the countryside, locating gold or silver ores. Its title 'Pneumatic Boots and Shoes', applied for by a Kingston barrister, acting as a patents agent and Nissen describes himself as a mechanical constructor, which reveals the nature of his employment at the Halifax engineering firm.

First a simple description:-

"My invention consists of a rubber bag or cushion inflated with air and fitted into the sole of a boot or shoe; the object of my invention is to increase the comfort in walking."

He then describes his drawing of the boot and its construction, followed by the really protective part of the patent, the claim or claims - Nissen had only one -

"What I claim as my invention and desire to procure by patent is the combination in the sole of the boot or shoe a rubber bag 'A' with a valve 'B', attached substantially as and for the purpose hereinbefore set forth." We may ignore the legal jargon which may confuse the correctness of the claim but we cannot discover whether the wearers of such boots carried with them an air pump ?

A more complicated patent was that of the original Nissen hut. It was patented in various countries and the one now quoted is from the patent applied for in March 1917, from the Registrar of Patents at Pretoria in South Africa, with the unpretentious title:-

'Improvements in and relating to portable buildings.'

152

The Memorial to fallen members of the Institution of Mining and Metallurgy, many of whom were Tunnellers in World War I.
(courtesy of the Institution of Mining and Metallurgy.)

Above. Falklands War 1982. Royal Engineers appear to be collecting stone to surface roads in front of the Nissen huts.
Below. A road already surfaced.
(Both photographs courtesy of the Royal Engineers Library, Chatham. Kent.)

154

Although the general nature of the Nissen hut is well known, the precise description, as worked out by the inventor and patent agent leaves us in no doubt about the essence of the invention:-

"This invention relates to portable buildings, of the bow or semicircular type, in which the roof extends to the floor and it has for its objects facilitating the standardisation of the parts, reducing the number of different parts to a minimum, limiting the sizes of the several parts for the purpose of facilitating transport, simplifying the work involved in setting up and taking down, reducing the total weight of the material to a minimum without impairing the strength and stability of the building, providing air spaces of maximum capacity between the inner and outer walls and obtaining a maximum floor space per unit of cost."

He then proceeds with a description of the invention accompanied by lettered diagrams, taking up several pages, after which came the claims, twelve of them.

"Having now particularly described and ascertained the nature of my said invention and in what manner the same is to be performed, I declare that what I claim is:-

1. A portable building having a frame formed of a series of bows or semicircular shaped ribs, each comprising three or more similar elements, a series of exterior purlins longitudinally arranged on and fused to said ribs and a series of corrugated iron sheets fixed to the said purlins."

Two of the succeeding 12 claims are as follows:-

2. In a portable building of the type specified in the preceding claim, forming the purlins in length and joining up said lengths at the intersection of the purlins with said ribs.

3. In a portable building of the type specified in the preceding claims, fixing the purlins to the ribs by means of hook bolts arranged in the manner specified."

And so each aspect of the original specification is emphasised in separate claims, to prevent anyone from infringing the patent and to the credit of Nissen and his patent agents there is no evidence of infringement and consequent court cases.

'Necessity, Mother of Invention...' wrote William Wycherley in his 1671 play, *Love in a Wood,* the wood being St James' Park in London ! - and it was necessity which brought about the invention of the Nissen Bow Hut, the Nissen Hospital Hut and the Nissen Steel Tent. An alternative Stamp Mill was more 'the power of novelty as an inducement to action' (Encycl. Brit.) than 'necessity' but it succeeded, partly because Head, Wrightson and Company of Stockton, had a workable cash flow, as well as the necessary expertise. Again, I shall lean on the Encyclopedia for a terse definition of the inventive process which at first sight may appear academic, yet on careful dissection can include the Pneumatic Boot, the Nissen Stamp Mill and the Nissen Huts:-

'an essential and continuing tension in higher organisms between the establishment and maintenance of environmental constancies and the interruption of achieved equilibria in the interest of new possibilities of experience.'

Which can simply be expressed as a break with tradition. Yet this statement does not explain the motivation of the inventor - what makes the inventor 'tick' ?

Research involves periods or wearisome searching among reliable - and sometimes, not so reliable - sources. The exploration of avenues leading to nothing whatsoever in an endeavour to discover who did it, how and where ? Such an occupation might seem unbearable, but for the occasional stroke of good luck which I had one winter's evening when tuning into Radio 4 BBC before the news and finding that I was listening to the end of a talk by Mike Burrows, the inventor of the Lotus monocoque bicycle. It will be remembered that this bicycle, of revolutionary design, was powered by Chris Boardman to an Olympic Gold Medal Victory at Barcelona. Burrows is an engineer and prefers this description to that of 'inventor' - he is on record as saying; "I hate the word 'inventor', adding quirkliy: ... an inventor tries to solve other peoples problems and an engineer only tries to solve his own ! And that is what I do." It appears that he would prefer the term 'innovative designer'.

Reviewing the previous paragraphs of this chapter and cogitating on Burrow's remarks in Radio 4, I realised that I was seeing only the tip of the invention iceberg and that there was more to it than the entry of the invention into the physical world, whilst the submerged portion of the invention iceberg had remained unrecognised and unexamined - well, almost ! He had, however,

156

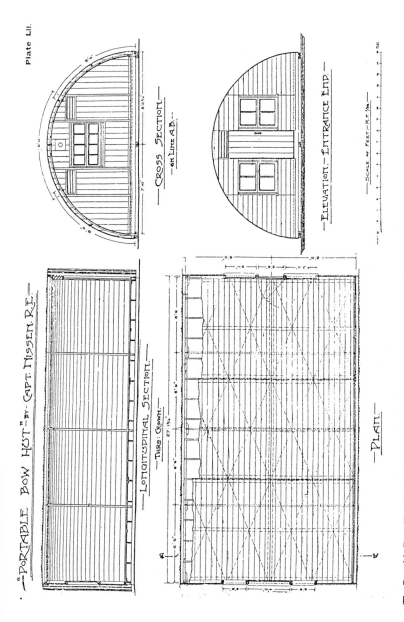

Plate LII.

The Portable Bow Hut: The diagram in the patent application submitted by Nissen to the South African Patent Office in Pretoria in 1917, No. 117/17. This was similar to diagrams in applications to patent offices in Great Britain (1916), Canada (1917) and the United States (1917).

157

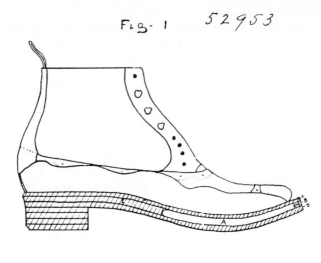

Fig. 1 52953

SECTION

Fig. 2

PLAN

Nissen's first patented invention was "Pneumatic Boots and Shoes" (July 1896 No. 52953, Canada). The valve 'B' enabled air to be pumped into the space 'A' which, he claimed, made for more comfortable walking. I have found no reference to the manufacture of such footwear.

158

mentioned some investigations on the subject at Loughborough University of Technology and so I contacted him and as a result I was sent some reports by Linda Candy, a Research Fellow, especially her *Mike Burrows: A Case Study in Innovative Design*. (March 1994) Again, we meet the term 'Innovative Design' which encapsulates a modern attitude towards the more popular expression 'inventor'. The extraction of gold particles from a rock by crushing with a hammer, or alternatively, by panning river silt, when the heavier gold particles sink to the bottom of the pan, might be termed 'invention', or even their subsequent extraction by mercury ? But later technological improvements, the use of a heavy wooden stamp, then the stamp shod with steel, the harnessing of water energy to a one stamp mill, then several stamp mills which called for a camshaft with cams for raising the stamps, followed by confining the process of ore-crushing to a mortar - all these were innovations on a single theme, the extraction of gold from its environment, a theme 'invented' perhaps by an unknown Saxony miner in the 16th century ? A dilemma, possibly, yet I fear that 'inventor' will never be supplanted in general use by 'innovative designer', but a compromise might be made regarding 'inventor' as a 'buzz' word, an example of technical jargon, implying various aspects of innovation ?

Linda Candy has not only investigated the evolution of the monocoque bicycle, but has made a parallel study of Mike Burrows' thoughts on how and why bicycle designs were adapted as a result of innovative studies arising from interviews with him. Briefly, to quote her: "The goal of the research was to describe, in the widest sense, how the designer generated ideas, developed them and brought them to fruition." Of special interest is her emphasis on biography and 'the formative influences that helped shape his character and working practice' because there are significant parallels between the early lives of Burrows and Nissen. A stable home life does not necessarily develop inventiveness, yet the similarities between their young lives are noteworthy, but more so the close industrial contact between father and son: Nissen and his mining engineer father and Burrows with his aeronautical engineer father. Peter and Georg Nissen co-operated and sometimes quarrelled, whilst producing the Stamp Mill. Richard Burrows, likewise, helped his son Mike in modelling the carbon fibre monocoque. A further result of what might be described as a technical psycho-analysis of Mike Burrows was that both received informal engineering apprenticeships in their father's workshops; both were in terms of the Chapter 3 title 'singular engineers'.

To anyone coming for the first time to this analysis of the inventor's motivation, there is a most enlightening section dealing with two aspects of invention referred to as 'product' and 'process', representing a 'principled design approach' in which these two aspects come to life as complementary design perceptives. Burrows reverted to the basic bicycle design as a mental launch pad for bicycle design, in which the usual design rules were broken. The tubular frame was disposed of in favour of a single carbon fibre shell, hence 'monocoque'. Construction was then restarted from a parallel series of designs, a process which illustrates the meaning of 'lateral thinking', a method of solving problems indirectly, or even illogically. Nissen, likewise, in 1916 at Ypres, must have appreciated the unsatisfactory nature of existing army huts, devices prepared from wood and canvas and started again from a parallel example, the skating shed at Queen's University, which he gradually redesigned in the three stages mentioned in a previous chapter but, as we can see, from an 1890 photograph of an ice-hockey rink, the semicircular Nissen hut may have been derived from a design not intended for warfare, unless ice-hockey can be so described !

So much for 'product' and now for the second aspect of invention, that of 'process', which in Burrows' case involved the development of craft skills of which two examples are modelling with carbon fibre and working with solid aluminium. This was a feature, among others, of the Nissen inventions. The Nissen Stamp Mill required the use of craft skills which both Georg and Peter Nissen had already acquired, whilst working at the mines, but Peter Nissen's method of connecting sheets of corrugated iron to form an interior lining to the Nissen hut demanded a new technique which he evolved, a technique which he later applied to the Nissen Steel Tent.

These brief notes on the nature of invention fail to do sufficient justice to the Loughborough research on the motivation of innovators, but whether there can be a generalised answer to the question; 'What makes inventors 'tick'? depends, I suggest, on further research directed towards other inventors, who are willing to speak their minds, a situation which pleases me, indicating as it does the ongoing nature of biography. How I envied his early life in North Carolina at a time when the world was still young.

Thus, only about 150 pages, the disappointing result of several years part-time research and, even now, I know so little about Peter Nissen. "How submerged does a reference have to be before it drowns ?" asks Julian Barnes, in the first chapter of his *Flaubert's Parrot*, a brilliant satire on the irrelevance of some biographical research. Even less would have been known about Peter Nissen but for that which was retrieved by Lauretta Nissen. Between us, many submerged references have been fished out of the sea of oblivion before they drowned. Yet, what I find extraordinary is the lack of recorded communication between Nissen and his first wife, Louisa, or with his daughter Betty. It is a story mainly about achievements, rather than personalities.

8. POSTSCRIPT AND AFTERTHOUGHTS

Nissen never received a civil honour; one might have hoped for a knighthood but it never happened. Did the acrimonious dispute with the War Office close the Establishment door on him ? We are unlikely ever to know the answer. A worse omission is his absence from the *Dictionary of National Biography* but it is hoped to see him in the *New DNB* now being compiled.

My anguished cry, "Oh for a German Corporal Donger '" in a previous chapter has since been answered by information contained in a little known but important book, *Architecture of Aggression* by Keith Mallory and Arvid Ottar, published in 1973 by the Architectural Press (now Butterworth Architecture.) It mentions two significant advantages held by German armies in 1917 which rendered unnecessary the provision of a massive hut system such as was required by the Allied troops. Firstly, the German armies had a regional advantage in which men and materials could be transferred to and from the fighting line without hindrance of the English Channel. Yet even more important - the German armies held the railway system of the region by which troops could be transported to where they were needed, and back again if necessary, a philosophy of lateral movement. The German approach to hutting is demonstrated by the provision of portable hangars for aircraft so that when the planes moved the hangars moved also. This contrasted with the use of Nissen huts which were capable of being dismantled, transported and then reassembled, yet it appears that they were rarely moved from one place to another.

The term 'Mass-production' is one which we usually associate with the motor industry and especially with Henry Ford who adopted the system in 1910. The component parts of the finished product must be simplified and standardised so that they can be easily fitted to other parts without time-wasting adjustment. Nissen's method of assembling his huts involved the production of 'components' at factories widespread throughout the United Kingdom which were shipped to France and thence to where they were required. There, with the aid of a spanner, they were assembled according to the instructions which accompanied each hut. As Henry Ford was a pioneer of car mass-production, so Peter Nissen was a pioneer of the mass-production of huts and the principle of 'prefabrication' which was continued after World War I and proved so technically sound in World War II.

Should we not remember him for his development of the Nissen Stamp-mill, the invention of the Nissen Hut and the concept of mass-produced houses ?

164

APPENDIX I

PATENTS REGISTERED BY PETER NORMAN NISSEN

These are classified by Number, e.g., 12345, and Year e.g., .04

GREAT BRITAIN

Nissen Stamp Mill	24266.10	
Nissen Stamp Mill	26745.10	
Stamp Mill, feeder drives	16282.12	
Centrifugal machines	8643.14	
Improvements to Stamp Mills	8964.16	
Portable Buildings	105468.16	The Nissen Hut
Joints for corrugated sheets	116546.17	
Improvements to Portable buildings	118442.18	
Portable Buildings	129777.19	The Nissen Steel Tent
Rick Shelters	152126.20	
Improvements to Portable Buildings	320132.29	

TRANSVAAL. (Prior to South African Act of Union, 1910)
Nissen Stamp Mill   465.05

SOUTHERN RHODESIA. (Later Rhodesia, now Zimbabwe)
Nissen Stamp Mill   878.12
Nissen Stamp Mill   879.12

SOUTH AFRICA.

Nissen Hut	110.17	
Joints for corrugated sheets	292.19	
Nissen Steel Tent	293.19	
Temporary Sheds & Shelters	294.19	

CANADA

Pneumatic Boots & Shoes	52953.96	
Nissen Hut	179087.17	
Nissen Steel Tent	194203.19	
Temporary Buildings & Shelters	194204.19	
Jointing Corrugated Sheets	194205.19	

UNITED STATES OF AMERICA

Ore Stamp MIll	776414.04	
Ore Stamp-mill Mortar	945135.10	Application in 1904
Ore Stamp Mill	111908.14	Application in 1908
Jointing Corrugated Sheets	1351435.20	
Portable Buildings	1377500.21	Application in 1917

APPENDIX II

PATENTS REGISTERED BY GEORG HERMAN NISSEN

UNITED STATES OF AMERICA

Windowblind Stops	174559.76	
Feed-bag for horse	729396.03	
Ore Stamp Mill Mortar	862098.07	Application in 1900

CANADA

Automatic Ore Feeders	65587.89
Ore Stamp Mill Mortars	69534.00

APPENDIX III

PETER NORMAN NISSEN

A TENTATIVE CHRONOLOGY

1871	Born New York, August 6th
1873	To Norway with parents and sister, Gurina (Ena) born 1869
1875	Returned to New York
1877	To Philadelphia, where brother Julius was born in March, thence via Georgia to High Point, North Carolina
1883	Moved to Thomasville
1887-1888	In preparatory department Trinity College
1889	Not at Trinity College, Home now in Albemarle Went to Nova Scotia with father
1890-1891	Attended academic course at Trinity College but left without taking a degree
1891	To Nova Scotia with family
1895	Sent by Halifax engineering firm to erect stamp-mill at Queen's University, Kingston, Ontario
1896	First patent issued July, No. 52953 (Canada) - 'Pneumatic Boots & Shoes"
1896-1897	At Queen's University doing 1st year Surveying in the School of Mining, where he was also a demonstrator
1897	Engaged to Louisa Mair Richmond
1898-1899	Developing the Hornblende Mine, Wawa, Ontario

1900	Married Louisa Richmond, January 2nd
1902	Birth of daughter, Elizabeth (Betty) at Kingston
1904	Nissen Stamp Mill patented in the United States Nos. 766414.04 and 945135 applied for, granted in 1910
1904-1907	Erecting mills in Idaho, Utah, Arizona and Mexico
1905	Nissen Stamp Mill patented in Transvaal, No. 465.05
1910	To the Witwatersrand, Transvaal, via the U.K.
1911-1912	Stamp mill discussions at meetings of the Chemical, Metallurgical and Mining Society of South Africa, Oct, Nov, and Dec, 1911 and Jan, Mar, 1912 about tests with the Nissen Stamp Mill at the City Deep Mine
1912	The Nissens return to England
1913-1914	Nissen forms Nissen's Ltd, a building contracting Company
1914 Aug	British declaration of war on Germany
1915 Jan	Temporary Lieut, Sherwood Foresters (Nottingham and Derbyshire Regiment)
1915 May	Temporary Lieut, Royal Engineers
1915 Aug	Temporary Capt, Royal Engineers
1916 Apr	Nissen at Ypres, Belgium, visualises semicircular hut
1916 Jun	Applied for patent for "Improvements in and relating to Portable Buildings". This was the Nissen Hut, patent No. 105468.16 (UK)
1916 Jul	Beginning of Somme battles
1916 Sep	Nissen Huts first used in France
1916 Nov	Acting Major
1917 Mar	Awarded the Distinguished Service Order (DSO) for inventing and supplying a new type of hutting.
1917 May	Acting Lieut Colonel

1917 Jun	Applied for patent for "Improvements in joints for corrugated sheets" (a method of joining corrugated iron sheets for hut linings.) Patent No. 116546.17 (UK)
1918 May	Temporary and Acting Major - Not a demotion, but command of a Royal Engineers unit to liaise with the newly formed Royal Air Force near Nancy, in the south of France
1918 Jul	Applied for patent for "Improvements in and related to Portable Building." This was the Nissen Steel Tent. No. 129777.19 (UK)
1919 Nov	In Foreign Orders List. St Sava 3rd Class (Serbia) My request for the citation has never been answered
1920 Jun	There is no date for Nissen's demobilisation as Lieut Colonel from the Army, but his last mention in the Army List was in June 1920
1921	National Wool Sheds built at Hull by Nissen's Ltd Becomes U.K. Citizen
1922	Nissen purchased the house 'Deepdale' on Westerham Hill, Kent. Louisa returns from the U.S.
1923	Death of Louisa Nissen, July 23rd
1925	Son born March 17th, Peter Charles Maitland
1930	Death of Peter Norman Nissen, March 2nd at 'Deepdale'. Son born March 29th, George Maitland Daughter, Elizabeth (Betty) Lavinia, leaves for California.

APPENDIX IV

BOOKS AND DOCUMENTS CONSULTED

PMN	Collection Peter Maitland Nissen
LN	Typed copy of written memoranda by Lauretta Nissen from Collection Peter Maitland Nissen

Chapter 1   PIONEERS ! O PIONEERS !

Encyclopaedia Britannica	15th Edition 1977, Vol 16 (Macropaedia) pp 312-328. Scandinavia, History of	
Arvid Midbrod	*Egersund* (Two A4 pages of the History of Egersund, in English)	Dalane Museum Egersund
G.B. Nissen & H. Nissen	*Slekten Nissen Fra Bov Sogn I Sonderiyland* pp73-78 (The Family Nissen)	Trondheim 1978
Alistair Cook	*America* pp 174-185 First paperback edition 1978	BBC
LN	Memo written in pencil by Georg Nissen	
PMN	Untitled notes on Georg Nissen	

Chapter 2   CAROLINA DAYS

H.T. Lefler & A.R. Newsome	*The History of a Southern State North Carolina.* Chaps 1,4,5.	Univ of N Carolina Press 1954, 3rd Ed 1973.
Reid Jones	Letter to Lauretta Nissen 15.1.31.	PMN

Chapter 3   A SINGULAR ENGINEER

Nora C. Chaffin	*Trinity College 1839-1892. The Beginnings of Duke University.* chaps 6,7,8,9	Duke Univ Press Durham, N.C. 1950
W.K. Boyd, ed.	*The Autobiography of Brantley York*	Trin. Coll. Hist. Soc. Durham, N.C. 1908-1909
A.L. Clark	*The First Fifty Years, A History of the Science Faculty at Queen's University. 1893-1943*	Queen's Univ Kingston, Ontario
The Mineral Industries Educational Trust	"Careers in Mining Engineering" "Undergraduates Courses" and syllabuses	6 St James Sq. London SW1Y 4ID
Countryside Campaigner	"Fatal Extractions" Mineral Extraction tearing the Heart from England.	CPRE, Warwick House 25 Buckingham Palace Road London
LN	Part II	

Chapter 4   THE NISSEN STAMP MILL

LN	Part II "The Stamp in South Africa"	
New Modderfontein Gold Mining Co Ltd	*The Gold Recovery Plant*	Transvaal Chamber of Mines 1921
Head, Wrightson & Co Stockton on Tees	*"Nissen Stamp Mills".*	1924
P.N. Nissen.	*Journal of the Chemical Metallurgy and Mining Society of South Africa*	Oct 1911, Nov 1911, Dec 1911, Jan 1912 and March 1912
T.K. Rose & W.A.C Neumann	*The Metallurgy of Gold*	Charles Griffin & Co 1937 7th Edition
A.P. Cartwright	*The Gold Miners*	Purnell & Sons, 1962 Johannesbsurg
LN	Memo written in pencil by Georg Nissen	
PMN	Photocopied memo "Head, Wrightson & Co"	Green Dragon Museum Local Studies Room Cleveland

Chamberlain & Co	Licence to sell Nissen's	Nissen Buildings Ltd
Lincoln's Inn	Stamp Batteries under	and P.N. Nissen, Esq
Solicitors (PMN)	Transvaal patent	Dated 11th July 1910

Chapter 5   FROM SKATING RINK TO NISSEN HUT

LN	Part III "The War"	
PMN	*Instructions for erecting*	Nissen Buildings Ltd
	16ft span Nissen Huts	Rye House, Hoddesdon
P.N. Nissen	Lt Col Nissen speaks to	*Queen's Journal*
	Engineering Society Queen's	Vol XLVI, *28*
	University, Kingston.	(3rd Feb 1920)
Director of Fortifications	Handbook of Nissen Huts	War Office E.10
and Works	16' and 24' Span. 1944 Ed.	Romney House
		Marsham Street
		LONDON SW1

Chapter 6   THE HUT LIVES ON

Croydon Local	"Death of ex-Mayor,Ald W.J.	*Croydon Advertiser*
Studies Library	Chamberlain's services to Croydon"	11th January 1930
PMN	*"Nissen" Patent Steel Buildings*	
	Nissen Steel Buildings	Reprint from *The British*
	for Industrial Purposes	*Engineer's Export Journal*
		Aug 1924
	Port of Hull Annual 1922. pp 4 & 31	
H.N. Appleby	*The Humber Ports"*	L.N.E.R. 1925
Australian Encyclopedia	"Wool". pp 353-354	
1968 edition		
PMN	*Nissen-Petren Houses 1925*	Nissen-Petren Houses Ltd
		25b, Queen Victoria Street
		LONDON EC4
South Somerset	Minutes - Housing Committee	17th Nov 1983, 2nd Feb 1984
District Council	Minutes - Planning Committee	8th Dec 1983
Jack Sweet	"Nissen council homes are	*South Somerset News*
	listed buildings."	*and Views.* Jan 1988
Phil Ault	"A Handy Guide to Iceland"	*The Saturday Evening Post*
		6th Feb 1943. pp20,21 & 63

Capt F.L. Oliver	"Iceland: Keystone for North Atlantic Defense"	*Christian Science Monitor* 8th July 1941
PMN	*The 'Nissen' Patent "Tukl"*	Nissen Buildings Ltd Hoddesdon. Herts
POW Chapel Preservation Committee	*Orkney's Italian Chapel*	Tourist Office, Kirkwall, Orkney
	"Britain's Strangest Church looks like a Cinema"	*The Sunday Referee* 1st March 1936
	Company Records Nissen Buildings Ltd on Microfiche	Companies House Crown Way, Cardiff CF4 3UZ

Chapter 7 NISSEN - MAN AND INVENTOR

| Linda Candy | "Mike Burrows: A Case Study in Innovative Design" March 1994 Ref 94/LUTCHI/0168 | Loughborough University of Technology |

APPENDIX V

THE GENEALOGY OF THE NISSEN FAMILY

Hinrich Lorenzen of Oldemoestoft	Born 1450 at Neumunster, described as Hunter at Copenhagen
Jacob Hinrich senior.	
Asmus Jacobsen	Born 1525, died 1654
Nis Asmussen	Born 1565
Lorentz Nissen	Born 1603, died 1654. About this time surnames seem to have got established, for all the rest are Nissens.
Nikolaus Nissen of Oldemoestoft	Born 1627, added Lerback and Rugballegaard, probably two more farms, to the property.
Nikolaus Nissen	Born 1660, seems to have been of some importance, he was "Councillor of Chancery", a legal post I suppose and later a judge. He married Elizabeth Sophie Hoegh, a lady who claimed descent from the ancient Kings of Denmark, Gorm and Harold Bluetooth, and Charlemagne through Berengaria of Portugal the very bad disagreeable Queen.

Christian Diltev Hoegh Nissen	Born 1690, Died 1775, was also a lawyer and manager of the Royal estates near Copenhagen. He married a French woman called Grandjean. She is reputed to have been very elegant and the small well shaped nose of which Peter Norman was so proud is supposed to have come from this French ancestress.
Mado Lind Nissen	Born 1756, is described as "mate on the ship Laurvigen". About 1794 he seems to have been appointed Commissioner at Egersund, a town in the south of Norway. There he married and died and this branch of the family became quite Norwegian.
Peder Lynge Nissen	Born 1797, at Egersund, was also a sailor and later Customs official at Kopervik, another town in Norway. He died there in 1881. He married Gurina Nissen and was Peter Norman's grandfather.
Georg Hermann Nissen	Born Egersund 1832, father of Peter Norman Nissen
Peter Norman Nissen	Born New York 1871, died Westerham, England, 1930. Three children, Elizabeth Lavinia, Peter Charles Maitland and George Maitland.

This genealogy, or 'pedigree' as she called it, was compiled by Peter Nissen's widow, Mrs Lauretta Nissen. The earliest dates refer to the farm Oldemoesoft and to one member born at Neumunster which is now in the Federal Republic of Germany, in the state of Schleswig-Holstein, annexed from Denmark in 1864. With German populations surrounded by Danes and Danish communities as minorities in German areas, Schleswig-Holstein has been noted for its complex history and its nationalistic tensions.